GET A
LIFE !

MOODY
to *mellow*

GET A LIFE!

MOODY to mellow

Stephen Palmer
and
Christine Wilding

Hodder Arnold

A MEMBER OF THE HODDER HEADLINE GROUP

Orders: Please contact Bookpoint Ltd, 130 Milton Park, Abingdon, Oxon OX14 4SB.
Telephone: (44) 01235 827720, Fax: (44) 01235 400454. Lines are open from 9.00 to 18.00, Monday
to Saturday, with a 24-hour message answering service. You can also order through our website
www.hoddereducation.com

British Library Cataloguing in Publication Data
A catalogue record for this title is available from the British Library.

ISBN-10: 0 340 90801 7
ISBN-13: 9 780340 908013

First published   2006
Impression number   10 9 8 7 6 5 4 3 2 1
Year   2008   2007   2006

Typeset by Pantek Arts Ltd, Maidstone, Kent.
Printed in Great Britain for Hodder Arnold, a division of Hodder Headline,
338 Euston Road, London, NW1 3BH, by Bath Press, Bath.

Hodder Headline's policy is to use papers that are natural, renewable and recyclable products and made
from wood grown in sustainable forests. The logging and manufacturing processes are expected to
conform to the environmental regulations of the country of origin.

Every effort has been made to trace copyright for material used in this book. The authors and
publishers would be happy to make arrangements with any holder of copyright whom it has not been
possible to trace successfully by the time of going to press.

CONTENTS

CONTENTS

DEDICATION

To my wonderful children, Leonie, Ross and Olivia, who have warmly supported me through many stressful moments in my own life!

Christine

To Maggie, Kate, Kevin, Tom, Arina and Joshua, who have all helped me at different times to manage my stress.

Stephen

INTRODUCTION

'The beginning is the most important part of the work.'
Plato, *The Republic*

The fact that you have taken the trouble to purchase and begin to read this book tells us that you consider yourself to be suffering from stress, and that you would seriously like to do something about it.

You have come to the right place! By the time you have worked through, with us, the 100 days of this book, you will be able both to deal with pressure and to banish stress – permanently.

We are not planning to be too easy on you, as we are going to make you work hard – though in an enjoyable and results-orientated way. This is not so much a book to read as a book of action. Using it on a daily basis – which we hope you will – you will be asked to devote between 5 and 30 minutes a day to practising and learning a new stress-busting skill. Each day's new learning is accompanied by an activity to keep you on your toes – and you have the option of signing up to have this activity re-enforced via a daily text message reminder. We would encourage you to sign up to this. It will almost be like having us personally encouraging you to keep going when you have decided that you are far too stressed out, over-busy and over-loaded to spare the time to work on stress management.

The activities are the most important part of the book, and if you are to become the mellowest person around, it is essential that you take them seriously and achieve them on a daily basis. We will never ask too much of you – sometimes an activity will require you to do little more than ensure you really understand your learning for the day. However, it is strongly preferable that you complete all the activities to achieve the desired results.

There is some further 'bad news' about the activities. They are not always 'one offs' – you can't think 'I only have to do it once and then I can forget about it'. Several (we don't want to frighten you off by saying 'many' – let's say, somewhere in between 'several' and 'many') of the points will be ongoing. This is because you will only internalise your new, mellower ways of being by making your activities your new default. As you will understand as you work on the exercises, we are also looking for patterns that are personal to you, and this kind of detective work only succeeds when you have a good many samples to analyse.

The good news is that, as we emphasise in other parts of the book, nothing that we ask of you will take that long (is 15 minutes OK?) nor will it be that difficult (if you are intelligent enough to be reading this book, the tasks will be easy and fun). We even anticipate possible withdrawal symptoms when you have worked through the entire book and feel so mellow that you are looking for something to do with your spare time!

One further thing: the programme is designed to turn your life around in 100 days – but of course, you can feel free to speed up or slow down, according to your time and your progress.

So, how do you use this book? First, you need some tools.

Ensure that, before you start, you have purchased a hard-covered A4 lined notebook, own a whole clutch of working pens, and have a safe, quiet personal place to keep them where they will not be pilfered by other members of the family or colleagues at work. We ask you to use a hard-cover notebook as this will definitely give more cohesiveness to the stress-busting work you are about to undertake. Don't give yourself further stress at this stage by having to look for your tools!

Once you have your tools to hand, take a look at the layout of this book. It is divided into ten chapters, each dealing with a different aspect of stress. Your own stress profile will be unique to you – what stresses you might have no impact at all on us, and the things that have us tearing our hair out may be things you deal with easily. So you may well wish to focus on those aspects that reflect your own most difficult personal problems.

There are 100 'days' in total (we agree - that's a lot of time and a lot of work). How can we do this to you when all you want is a quick fix? Well, we're doing it because quick fixes don't last. Like plasters, they peel off before long.

So stick with us, because if you do, you really will get your life back on track – permanently – and it will be richer, happier, and more fun.

We promise you now:

- Stress-busting will be interesting.
- Some of it will even be fun.
- We will spell things out in a punchy, common-sense way that you will grasp speedily and easily.
- You will see excellent results quickly.
- You will become an expert on de-stressing.
- We will stay alongside you every step of the way.
- Life will be so much better by the end of all your hard work.

To begin with, we need to make sure that you understand just what stress is and have a good working knowledge of when it is good for you (yes, really, it is, sometimes!) and bad for you, what brings it on and what you might be doing (unknowingly) to encourage it. In a sense, before you start, you need to know your enemy. Once we are confident that you are an expert in understanding it, we give you every strategy you could possibly need to deal with it.

Let's get going!

Stephen Palmer and Christine Wilding

Daily Text Message Service

 A unique, interactive text messaging service is available★ with this book. Daily texts provide inspiration as well as key tips and advice to help you achieve your goal.

By subscribing at the beginning of a 10-day period you will receive a message each day encouraging you and supporting the guidance already given in the book for that day.

So, what are you waiting for? Text the keyword on Day 1 to 80881 to receive invaluable advice that will help you to achieve your full transformation.

★ UK only

CHAPTER 1

UNDERSTANDING STRESS

What is stress?

Stress. We talk about it, read about it, struggle with it – but what is it, exactly? It is certainly one of the most commonly used words in the English language.

> **Today you will learn ...**
>
> that the more you know about your enemies, the easier it is to overcome them. In this case, the enemy is stress.

Do you know anyone who is not stressed? In this day and age, we tend to look askance at the person who tells us that they do not suffer from stress. How can that be? Are they not living their life in the full-tilt, head-on, fast-lane way that we are programmed to believe is the true way to fulfilment and reward?

Whilst we hope you will think this is the best book you have found on stress, it certainly isn't the first on the subject. Stress advice can be found:

◆ In bookshops
◆ On television chat shows
◆ In magazine articles
◆ In chemists' shops
◆ Over the garden fence
◆ And, more and more commonly, in doctors' surgeries.

What is your view of stress? Get out your brand new, probably as yet unused hard-cover A4 notebook and write down what being, or feeling, stressed means to you. (If you don't have your book ready, then write your definition in the box below – and make getting your notebook a priority!)

My personal definition of stress is ...

_____

_____

_____

UNDERSTANDING STRESS

Let's see if your suggestions match ours. One way we see stress is as a reaction that comes along when your ability to cope is not equal to the situations that must be coped with.

'Stress occurs when perceived pressure exceeds perceived ability to cope.' Palmer

TOP TIP

- Keep in mind the importance of that word **perceived**. More on this later.

We also like the type of definition you may already have taped up on your office wall, and which can be purchased on postcards in high street shops, which goes along the lines of:

'Stress is created when your mind overrides the body's natural desire to choke the living daylights out of an idiot who is driving you completely crazy.'

However, stress can also be created by events which are outside our control. Sometimes we give a personal meaning to such events that is at best negative, at worst catastrophic. In these cases it is not our inability to cope that stresses us, but our lack of control over the situation.

TOP TIP

- Stress tends to occur when the 'To Do' pile exceeds our perceived coping skills.

Activity
What sort of stress?

- Look back at any stressful situations in the last week. Jot them down if you have the time. (Shorthand will do.) Now write next to each one, either 'WC' (within my control) of 'OC' (outside my control).

- Where does the balance lie? Are there more situations than you had imagined that were actually within your control?

UNDERSTANDING STRESS

'Don't assume it's impossible because you find it difficult. But recognise that if it's humanly possible, you can do it.'
Marcus Aurelius, Roman Emperor and stoic philosopher

Can I control the stress in my life?

You can! In yesterday's exercise, did you find that your own definitions were not too different from ours? What this means is that you actually know quite a lot about stress already.

> **Today you will learn ...**
>
> that much stress is self-induced, and that this is actually a **good** thing. Read on ...

The important points here are:

- An understanding that **you** have to take responsibility for the stress in your life
- Apply what you will learn in this book – don't just read it through, nod sagely, and put it back on the shelf
- **Get active** – this will make the difference.

These points are vital to take on board as the most important element in relieving stress is simply increasing your awareness of how you react to certain situations.

For the majority of us, the truth is that a great amount of the inappropriate, unhealthy stress we encounter is self-induced. This sounds harsh, but the fact that stress is within your control is actually a good thing.

⊙ TOP TIP

- ♦ Increasing our awareness of how we react to stress is half the battle.
- ♦ Much day-to-day stress in our lives is self-induced.
- ♦ This is good news for those who have decided to get rid of stress for good. It will be easier than you think.

We are of course not talking about life's genuine traumas, which are far outside the remit of this book. Here, we are considering, and intending to help you with, the common-or-garden stress that seems to blight our lives daily both at home and at work.

Activity
What's causing your stress

- ● Think of the most recent situation when you felt **really** stressed. Get out your notebook and write it down.

- ● Now write down what you believe to be the cause of your stress in relation to that incident. Was it due to something outside your control, or was there perhaps an element in your thinking that said, 'I can't cope with this'?

UNDERSTANDING STRESS

Why me?

> ### Today you will learn ...
>
> to focus in on, and identify, specific stress triggers (stressors) that are personal to you.

As mentioned in the introduction, we all have our own personal stress profiles. You may notice this most commonly at work, or in family situations. Something that really works you up may have little effect on your partner or colleague (and that can work you up even more)!

Now that you have a generic model for stress, and some ideas about what it is, you need to develop a stress profile that is specific to you.

This is really important, as you are going to take responsibility for working on the issues that have the most effect on your particular life. There is no point in us giving you advice on overcoming the type of issues that stress **us** out, as these may be things that scarcely cause your breath to quicken.

Learning to identify your own stress triggers is a very important skill.

Stress can be either:

◆ Chronic (like a nagging tooth-ache that we intend to find time to deal with, but almost learn to live with meanwhile) or
◆ Acute (when we have such a severe bodily reaction to something that our coping mechanisms pack up immediately).

Stress hangs around in both these forms much of the time, and you need to start identifying what precipitates a stress reaction for you.

Tomorrow's activity is to begin to keep a stress journal. As you gather more entries, you will begin to see a pattern of the particular things that leave you feeling most stressed out. For today, we are going to concentrate on stress triggers and stress outcomes.

To begin with, you need to identify triggers alone. Simply draw a line down a page of your notebook or make a chart like the one shown here. Record a few events when you felt stressed. What do you think it was that caused the stress (your views may change as you work through this book, but this will get you going)?

UNDERSTANDING STRESS

Remember, stress triggers are usually the things that push you over the edge when you were struggling to hang on by your fingertips in any event.

Event	Stress trigger
Piles of work on desk.	Boss asked me when it would all be done.
Rushing to leave work on time to see football on TV.	Wife calls to say, 'Could you collect daughter from friend's.'

As you fill in the columns, you will begin to see just what makes you feel you have simply lost the plot. Notice whether these are major events or minor irritations. This will also help you recognise how stressed you are.

TOP TIP

- We all have personal stress profiles.
- This explains why we can get upset by something that doesn't bother a friend at all.
- Learning about your own profile is a key to dealing with your stress.

Activity

Your personal stressors

- Begin to think more about specific personal stressors, rather than simply accepting stress as a generic part of life.

- Note down any patterns that seem to occur. Are you always stressed early in the morning? Why might this be?

UNDERSTANDING STRESS

How much does stress affect you?

> **Today you will learn ...**
>
> the helpfulness of rating stress.

If you are still reading, then you obviously feel that stress does affect you. The question is – how much? A simple way to work this out it simply to rate it.

Today you will start becoming familiar with the idea of rating your stress. Whether your stress is appropriate or not (see Day 5) often depends less on the situation itself, and more on how stressful you, personally, see it.

For example, if you are waiting on a street corner for a friend who fails to appear, of course that will be extremely frustrating. Just how frustrating it seems will be dependent on many factors, including your own personal tolerance levels. More about this later, but for the moment, we want you to start giving a PSR (Personal Subjective Rating) to your stress levels. This is also going to be a great tool for predicting patterns.

Use a 1–10 scale.

> PSR1 = scarcely bothered at all
> PSR10 = incandescent with frustration

Take heed of the P for personal and S for subjective. This is not higher mathematics – it is simply about how you feel at the time – so go with your immediate gut reaction and record it.

Today you are going to begin your stress journal. You can use the presentation shown here, or adapt it for yourself if you prefer a different layout. You are most welcome to photocopy our chart if you wish. We have given you a few examples to start you off.

Don't elaborate in the 'How did I feel?' column, just choose one of the following: anxious, annoyed, upset, distressed, angry, worried.

These will quite adequately describe your stress in most situations. (We are just looking for patterns at present, not detail.)

We will be adding more detail to this journal in later chapters, so stick with it as a simple tool for the moment, whilst you get used to stress awareness and rating its severity.

What happened? (My stress trigger)	When? (Date and time)	How did I feel? (My stress outcome)	PSR (Rate how I felt)
Locked self out of house.	8.30 pm Monday	Furious, anxious	8
Train to work $\frac{1}{2}$ hr late.	7.45 am Tuesday	Annoyed, frustrated	6
New work project 'dumped' on me – impossible deadline.	12.15 pm Wednesday	Worried, anxious	7
Now start to fill in your own examples of stress in your journal			

Keep this diary for at least two weeks – until you begin to notice patterns.

- ◆ Do you get more stressed at certain times of day?
- ◆ Do certain people seem to trigger more stress?
- ◆ Do stressful situations arise more in your workplace, home or social situations?
- ◆ Are there any particular connections that you can make? For example, you get more annoyed by events after a couple of drinks.

Activity

Start your stress journal

- ● Get your notebook and pen, and start your stress journal. One item per day will be enough – but you can write down as many as you wish.

- ● What patterns, if any, are you noticing? Write them down.

Is all stress bad?

There is a common view that stress is a **bad** thing. This idea causes us to worry about it even more, as we absolutely don't want bad things in our lives and set about rectifying the position.

> **Today you will learn ...**
>
> that some stress is actually good.

On the other hand, we often hear people say:

◆ 'I thrive on stress.'
◆ 'Stress is what motivates me.'
◆ 'I do my best work when I am really stressed.'

Does this mean that stress can sometimes be a good thing?

Actually, it does. Good stress – or, more accurately, 'pressure' as we'll be calling it from now on (though if you want to sound very clever, you can call it 'eu-stress') – is what motivates us to stretch ourselves mentally and physically. It is what ensures that we get up in the morning, achieve our goals during the day, do our best to win at tennis, ensure that our children are loved and safe. These challenges are necessary for us all, to ensure that we grow and develop both ourselves and others.

Bad stress (which can also be called 'distress'), on the other hand, makes us feel swamped and incapable: it leaves us feeling anxious and depressed and takes much of the joy from our lives. While pressure encourages us to achieve more, bad stress usually manages to get us to achieve less.

How do we know whether the personal stress that we feel is helping us or hindering us?

Yesterday we looked at rating our stress levels. We now need to work out whether these rates show our stress to be appropriate or inappropriate to the situation. It is inappropriate stress that we are more concerned with and are determined to ensure you get rid of.

Write down what you think decides whether stress is good for you or bad for you.

Let's see whether your answer matches ours …

In day-to-day stressful situations, it is largely how you view an event that determines whether it is placing you under pressure or bad stress. No single situation categorically leads to bad stress. It is your perception of the event that decides whether the stress is good or bad.

You'll learn lots of skills for ensuring that you turn bad stress into challenging pressure or no stress at all in later chapters of the book. For the moment, your goal is to understand the principles.

TOP TIP

♦ Pressure can be good for us and improve our motivation.

Activity

Positive and negative reactions to stress

● Take a page in your notebook and draw a line down the middle. Reflect on the times you have felt really stressed over the last week or two.

● On the left of the page, jot down stressful situations which caused you to react positively.

● On the right-hand side, write down stressful situations that you have reacted to negatively.

● What does the page look like?

● What does this tell you about your reactions to stress?

UNDERSTANDING STRESS

11

But I'm under more pressure than you!

Actually, that's **not** what makes the difference! It is quite normal for us to view our own situation as being 'harder', 'different' or whatever, in order to justify why we are more affected by stress than the next person.

> **Today you will learn ...**
>
> that our reaction to a situation can be more important than the situation itself.

So read the following story, and then we'll look at that again.

CASE STUDY

Jim and Peter both worked for the same organisation at the same level, although in different departments. On 'nodding' terms in the corridor, they did not really know each other. When a promotional opportunity came up, being reasonably ambitious, they both decided, independently, to apply for it. They were not alone. As it was an interesting job with a good salary, seven people in total tried out for the job.

After two rounds of interviews, the successful candidate was announced. It was neither Jim nor Peter. Both felt frustration and disappointment, and went home to re-think their positions.

Jim felt despairing. The whole process of applying for the position, the interviews and tests, the humiliation of rejection, the idea that he was obviously a poor employee who would never move up the company was so stressful to Jim that he felt totally exhausted and depressed and decided never to put himself though the experience again. Jim continued to work in the same department for the next seven years until he was, in fact, made redundant three years ago.

Peter also felt dreadful. He had found the whole process just as stressful as Jim. However, when he thought about it further he realised that of course moving up in such a good organisation was not going to be easy. He resolved to discover what skill deficits had prevented him from being promoted, and to see whether, through extra training or self-learning, he could do something about it. He also never wanted to go through such a stressful experience again, and decided that the answer was obviously to be better prepared next time.

Peter got his promotion next time around, is still working for the company, and was in fact the manager responsible for telling Jim that he was being made redundant three years ago.

If we were able to speak to Jim or Peter now, their views would probably be very different. Jim would no doubt say that the stress he experienced was a bad thing, and had a negative effect on his life. Peter, however, would say that the stress he experienced was a catalyst for change, as it showed him that he had to strive harder in order to achieve the success that he acquired.

Peter   Jim

TOP TIP

- In any given situation, you can **choose** how to react.
- The difference between pressure and stress (in regular, day-to-day situations) lies in your perception of the meaning of events, not the events themselves.
- You can turn your stress into pressure without avoiding stressful events.

Activity

Could you react more positively?

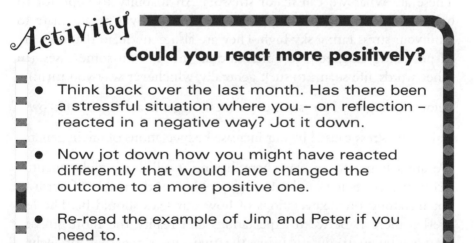

- Think back over the last month. Has there been a stressful situation where you – on reflection – reacted in a negative way? Jot it down.

- Now jot down how you might have reacted differently that would have changed the outcome to a more positive one.

- Re-read the example of Jim and Peter if you need to.

UNDERSTANDING STRESS

Major stress triggers

In general terms, what do you think are the major causes of stress in our society today?

Where do you think that your own stress especially comes from?

Today you will learn ...

about major stress triggers and their effect on your life.

Perhaps you are not quite sure – or haven't really thought about it. Being 'stressed out' is perhaps just something that you feel on an on-going basis without stopping to look at its specific causes – your personal 'stressors'.

Today you are going to look at some of the most common causes of stress, and think carefully about whether they apply to you. Your first steps to banishing stress will be made much easier if you know what your key personal stressors are.

First, do you have worries in any of the following areas?

◆ Your job
◆ Your relationship
◆ Your health
◆ Your finances

◆ Your family
◆ Your social life
◆ Losing a loved one.

These are what we call major stressors. An inability to cope (or to believe you can cope) in any one of these areas will be adequate to send your stress rating sky high. They are also generic, in that they are all-pervading and seem to be around all the time in some cases. (In other words, life seems to suck generally, whichever way you turn.)

Before moving on, there is one other stress trigger in a category of its own.

This is the stress caused by our increased expectations of life in general.

We are a living in an era where 'having it all' is a popular mantra. Accepting this belief can lead to the problem of the reality of our lives not matching our expectations of how our lives should be. The less overlap there is between expectations and reality, the more stressed we become in trying to bring the two closer together, or feeling frustrated that we cannot.

UNDERSTANDING STRESS

Check out what having it all means to you. What do you want most out of life? What are you either aspiring to achieve, or pedalling fast to ensure you maintain?

Now continue in your notebook, until you have 10 different 'having it all' expectations.

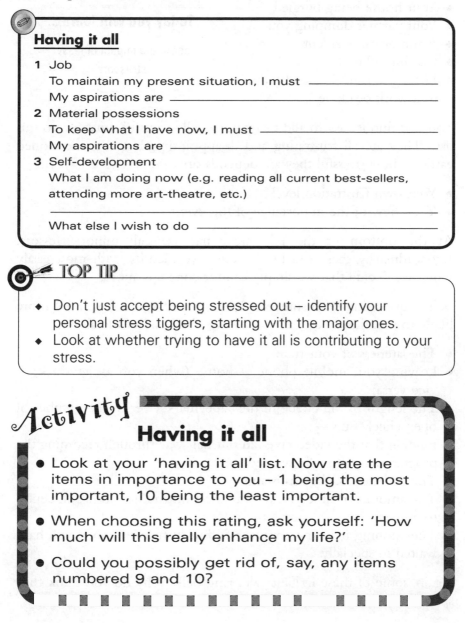

Having it all

1 Job
  To maintain my present situation, I must _____
  My aspirations are _____
2 Material possessions
  To keep what I have now, I must _____
  My aspirations are _____
3 Self-development
  What I am doing now (e.g. reading all current best-sellers, attending more art-theatre, etc.)
  _____
  What else I wish to do _____

TOP TIP

◆ Don't just accept being stressed out – identify your personal stress tiggers, starting with the major ones.
◆ Look at whether trying to have it all is contributing to your stress.

Activity Having it all

● Look at your 'having it all' list. Now rate the items in importance to you – 1 being the most important, 10 being the least important.

● When choosing this rating, ask yourself: 'How much will this really enhance my life?'

● Could you possibly get rid of, say, any items numbered 9 and 10?

UNDERSTANDING STRESS

Lesser stress triggers

Underneath the major stressors are two levels of lesser stressors. Firstly what we call mid-range stressors. These consist of very specific events, and might include the following:

◆ Your house being burgled
◆ Your partner dumping you
◆ A minor car accident
◆ Catching the 'flu
◆ Having to cancel a holiday due to a work deadline.

> **Today you will learn ...**
>
> about the impact of lesser stressors.

You will find it easy to add many personally stressful situations to this list. They are all frustrating and disappointing, but – as mentioned earlier – how stressful they are depends on:

◆ Your own frustration level
◆ Your view of the importance of the event.

At the bottom of the pile are what we call minor stressors. Extraordinarily, these can be the ones we identify with most easily when we decide that we simply cannot cope any more.

When discussing with someone how stressed you are, you are more likely to mention one of the following, than one of the above.

◆ The lateness of your train
◆ Leaving your mobile phone at home (when you are at work, or vice versa)
◆ The length of the queue in the supermarket versus the number of open check-outs
◆ Finding that the video tape ran out half way through recording the programme you really wanted to watch
◆ The rudeness of shop assistants
◆ The amount of time you have to wait on the line for a call centre to answer
◆ The washing machine engineer failing to turn up when you have waited in specially.

Again, some of these irritants will ring bells. Why do you think they spring to mind more quickly than the more major stressors?

UNDERSTANDING STRESS

Well, it is rather 'the straw that breaks the camel's back' principle coupled with the 'recency' principle. You struggle but manage, struggle but manage – and then the train to work is cancelled. This seems to finish you off, and is the most recent stressor you remember when asked why you look so frazzled and fed up.

It is important to understand this, as when we are looking for sources of stress, we need to look beyond the quick-fire stressors.

For example, whilst you may tell your partner or work colleague that the train being late made you feel so stressed out you could have cried / punched the announcement board, or whatever, you are not really telling it how it is. The chances are that the genuine cause was either a mid-range stressor (perhaps a holiday cancelled for work reasons) or a major stessor (perhaps the whole work situation).

So work as a whole is what needs to be looked at and possibly restructured to reduce the stress.

TOP TIP

- ◆ For all of us, major concerns seem to provide chronic stress, whilst small, one-off irritants tend to light the fuse that causes a stress explosion.
- ◆ We need to check for major stressors, rather than constantly trying to deal with lesser stressors.

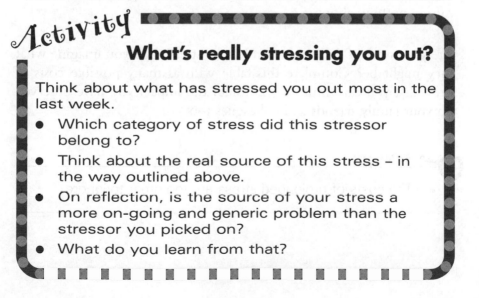

Activity **What's really stressing you out?**

Think about what has stressed you out most in the last week.

- Which category of stress did this stressor belong to?
- Think about the real source of this stress – in the way outlined above.
- On reflection, is the source of your stress a more on-going and generic problem than the stressor you picked on?
- What do you learn from that?

UNDERSTANDING STRESS

Managing stress: is it really necessary?

Managing stress can involve quite a lot of work initially until your new 'Mellow Defaults' kick in. Like going on a diet, we start off enthusiastically, but as we get hungrier and hungrier, our resolve weakens and we begin to tell ourselves that perhaps we are not so overweight after all.

> **Today you will learn ...**
>
> the costs of ignoring stress and the many benefits of managing it (both of which may be more than you realised).

This is the time for reinforcements! Today you are going to consider the costs of stress. Fold down a corner of this page or, better still, make one or two photocopies that you can place in your diary and magnet to the fridge.

We need to emphasise that when we discuss many of the costs of stress, we are talking about severe, prolonged stress over a long period of time. We are not concerned with the odd quickened heartbeat when you have to give a presentation, or the creeping anxiety you feel when you don't get a response to your job application. We are talking about stress over a long period that you choose to ignore, or think you can do nothing about.

Are you aware of the costs of prolonged stress? Can you imagine what they might be? Complete this table with as many possible costs of stress that you can think of – consider the impact you have observed on your family, friends and colleagues too.

TOP TIP

♦ The costs of prolonged stress are too great to ignore.

Cost of stress upon me	Cost of stress upon others I know

Activity

Remember the costs of stress

- During the day, be alert for other costs of stress you may have overlooked. Note them down in your notebook.

- Read through the costs at least three times to ensure that you are familiar with them and can bring them to mind easily.

UNDERSTANDING STRESS

Yes! Managing stress is really necessary

With your list on the table, let's take a look at how it matches with ours. There will be some costs (many, probably) that you had not thought of but, equally, you may have thought of some others not on the list below. Does the sheer number of negatives surprise you?

> **Today you will learn ...**
>
> that you ignore stress
> at your peril!

Here is our list.

Physical costs

- High blood pressure leading to increased risk of heart attack
- Exhaustion
- Weakened immune system leading to increased risk of illness
- Whilst not proven, research is looking at links between stress and an increased risk of cancer.

Psychological costs

- Low mood
- Depression
- Anxiety
- Sexual difficulties
- Impaired cognition (clear thinking)
- Sleep difficulties.

Social costs

- Relationship difficulties
- Loss of self-esteem
- Work difficulties including increased absenteeism that could lead to lower productivity, or even job loss
- Weakening of social links due to tiredness.

UNDERSTANDING STRESS

You need to consider this in a positive way, so let us now look at the benefits of managing stress.

First off, cover over the rest of this page and write down for yourself as many benefits as you can think of.

In a way, of course, this is quite easy. We suspect you have simply reversed the costs of stress to discover the benefits of managing it. However, we still intend to print them up boldly, so that they are writ large for you, and want to ask you to refer to them regularly – each time, in fact, that you put this book to one side and feel that the effort is too much. We hope this reminder will consistently get you back on track.

The benefits of stress management

- Physical good health, including
  - a strong immune system
  - lowering of your risk of illness
  - lowering of your risk of heart problems
- Psychological wellness including
  - good mood, ability to relax
  - clearer thinking and better memory
  - high self-esteem
- Improved social relationships
- Improved workplace relationships and productivity.

Activity

Remember the benefits of stress management

- Photocopy the benefits of stress management and ensure that you place the list where you can review it constantly.

- Read through both the costs and benefits at least three times to ensure that you are familiar with them and can bring them to mind easily.

UNDERSTANDING STRESS

Your notes

....

....

....

....

....

....

....

....

....

....

....

....

....

....

....

....

....

2

MEASURE AND MONITOR YOUR STRESS LEVELS

Are you keeping up? Do you need some help? If you've not already subscribed, why not try the daily text messaging service for extra encouragement and support. Just text 'Mellow 11' to 80881 now.

Each set of messages costs £1.50. Please see page xii for full terms and conditions.

Signs and symptoms of stress

> **Today you will learn ...**
>
> to spot the physical signs of stress easily.

Learning to recognise the signs and symptoms of stress is an important skill. If you can react quickly at the first signs of stress you will be able to nip it in the bud before it gets to a stage where it can seriously harm you or cause you to act in a destructive way. By the time you have read this book you will have a whole toolbox full of skills to help you deal with these symptoms.

What are you looking for?

Common signs and symptoms of stress fall into three categories:

- Physical signs
- Behavioural signs
- Psychological signs.

Today and tomorrow we will look at these more closely.

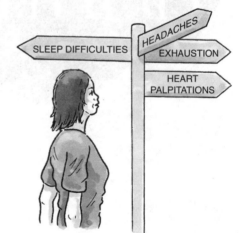

Physical signs and symptoms

Physical symptoms of stress range from minor, scarcely noticeable responses like feeling tired to the most dramatic of all, a heart attack. The longer you have been labouring under stress, the greater the likelihood of a more major problem.

Think about what happens when you are overwhelmed by stress. How do you feel physically? You will probably have no trouble picking out some of the many possible symptoms listed here.

MEASURE AND MONITOR YOUR STRESS LEVELS

Do you ever suffer from any of the following?

- Sleep difficulties
- Change in your eating patterns (stuffing, starving)
- Going to the loo every two minutes
- Loss of interest in sex
- Feeling exhausted, even though you only got up half an hour ago
- Heart palpitations
- Headaches or migraines
- Muscular tension.

These are some of your 'alert signals' and you need to start playing detective, rather than simply accepting them as a fact of life. In later chapters of this book you will learn techniques to relieve or remove all of the above symptoms. Once you have learned these skills you will be able to nip physical stress symptoms in the bud very quickly.

TOP TIP

- Never just accept physical symptoms. If you get a clean bill of health at the doctor's, don't just ignore things – look for stress-related reasons that you might be feeling this way.

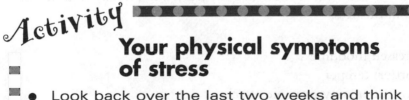

Activity

Your physical symptoms of stress

- Look back over the last two weeks and think about any physical problems you may have had that cannot be explained away. A broken arm due to a rugby tackle doesn't count, but being inexplicably exhausted by 7 pm each night might be worth further examination.

- Write these items down in your notebook. Now think about a possible explanation and write that down as well. Stress might be the answer ... you will find out over the coming days.

MEASURE AND MONITOR YOUR STRESS LEVELS

More signs and symptoms

Hopefully, yesterday's activity didn't turn you into a hypochondriac, but made you more aware of how stress shows itself.

> **Today you will learn ...**
>
> to spot the psychological and behavioural signs of stress.

Let's look now at the psychological and behavioural signs and symptoms of stress.

Such symptoms may not be noticed by you – often it is your friends, family or work colleagues who point them out to you. It is not until someone mentions your current moodiness, for example, that you become aware of it yourself. So when assessing these symptoms, do take heed of what others have to say. In fact, it is worth asking yourself, 'Have I been unusually short-tempered recently?' – and give a response of 'yes' or 'no'. If the answer is, 'You are always that way. What's new?' then it's time for anger management classes!

Have you noticed, or have your friends pointed out to you, any of the following? Remember that this is against a baseline of what is normal for you – if you've always bunked off work a lot, it may well not be a symptom of stress!

- Increased moodiness
- Short(er) temper
- Constant anxiety or panic attacks
- Finding it hard to get up in the mornings
- Frequently bunking off work
- Making silly mistakes due to poor concentration
- Feeling – or telling colleagues/friends – that you just can't cope
- Even the funniest jokes fail to amuse you
- You'd prefer to stay home than join the party.

The list isn't exhaustive – and nor is yesterday's list of physical symptoms. Everyone is different, but these are the sorts of things you should look out for. If a lot of the points apply to you, it is time to act. Don't ignore what your mind and body are telling you.

TOP TIP

- Listen to your friends. If they tell you that you are behaving like a bad-tempered grouch, don't think 'it's them' – it may be you, and it may be an important signal.

When you feel stressed, what symptoms alert you first? Do you feel it in your body, or in your mind? Take your notebook and write down the symptoms that especially apply to you. These will become your 'red alerts' – the signals that warn you that you need to do something positive as soon as you can.

TOP TIP

- Your red alerts can help you to resolve matters before the results become too serious.
- Identifying those that are personal to you is a powerful skill.
- The more familiar you become with your own particular stressors, the more quickly you will be able to spot them and act on them.

Activity **Identifying symptoms**

- How confident do you now feel about identifying stress-related symptoms? You have written them in your notebook and you have read about them above. Can you pinpoint them mentally, quickly and easily? Do you also understand why this is such important skill?

MEASURE AND MONITOR YOUR STRESS LEVELS

Take a stress test

> **Today you will learn ...**
>
> to measure your stress in an accurate way.

Before you go any further, you really do need to know just how stressed you are, and how it shows up in your life. If you're reading this book, you must already know that you are suffering from stress – but today's test will give you a more specific, objective rating for your stress overall.

Doing this test will help you rate your stress, notice patterns that are specific to you, and hopefully give you both information and reassurance. You might even find that your stress levels are lower than you thought!

Over time, you should notice a reduction in your stress levels. Make some copies of the test and re-take it on a monthly basis, to help you quantify your progress.

For each characteristic, give a rating of between 0 and 3.

0 = not at all
1 = rarely
2 = somewhat
3 = a lot

Total your scores at the end of each section.

This will show you two things: first, how stressed you are (the higher the score, the more you are suffering from stress) and second, whether your stress shows up in specific ways.

TOP TIP

- ◆ Stress shows up in a variety of ways. Using a stress test can help you to identify these signs.

Psychological stress response

I notice that I get (feel/suffer from)

Angry ☐	Anxious, apprehensive, frightened ☐
Ashamed, embarrassed ☐	Depressed, feeling low ☐
Guilty ☐	Jealous ☐
Moody ☐	Low self-esteem ☐
Feeling out of control ☐	Suicidal ideas ☐
Feeling helpless ☐	Paranoid thinking ☐
Unable to concentrate ☐	Intrusive images, thoughts, daydreaming ☐

Total score ....

Behavioural stress response

I notice that I get (feel/suffer from)

Passive or aggressive behaviour ☐	Compulsive or impulsive behaviour ☐
Irritability ☐	'Checking' rituals ☐
Increased alcohol consumption ☐	Increased caffeine consumption ☐
Comfort eating ☐	Increased time off from work ☐
Poor sleeping ☐	Withdrawing or sulking ☐
Increasingly accident prone ☐	Lack of interest in sex ☐
Showing anger (banging with fists, etc.) ☐	Speaking too much or too quickly ☐

Total score ....

Physical stress response

I notice that I get (feel/suffer from)

Frequent colds or other infections ☐	Indigestion ☐
Palpitations, or loud heartbeat ☐	Diarrhoea ☐
Breathlessness ☐	Constipation ☐
Tightness in chest ☐	Skin allergies ☐
Feeling faint or fainting ☐	Excessive sweating or clamminess ☐
Migraines ☐	Tension headaches ☐
Vague 'aches and pains' ☐	Rapid weight change ☐
Backache ☐	Menstrual problems, cystitis ☐

Total score ....

Total score for all three sections ....

Activity

Stress test

- Make sure you have done the stress test.
- Make a note in your diary to re-take it in a month's time.

MEASURE AND MONITOR YOUR STRESS LEVELS

How stress can make you sick

Over the last two days, we have looked at some of the costs of stress – many of them are physical. Some are more serious than others. Not all would actually be caused by stress – but stress could definitely make these problems worse and/or prolong them.

> **Today you will learn ...**
>
> not to ignore physical signs and symptoms of stress.

TOP TIP

- Too many of us take medication to reduce stress when we should be looking at lifestyle changes. Physical exercise, in particular, can help.

Pill-popping stress relief

Every week several million people take some form of medication for stress-related illness. It is just possible that you are one of them. This is not especially surprising given the very wide range of physiological changes that stress is capable of eliciting within our bodies.

Add to this the psychological changes – depression and a range of anxiety disorders – and that is a lot of sickness.

One of the biggest killers of the day is heart disease – and stress is regarded as a highly significant factor. We all know to not smoke, to watch what we eat and to take exercise, but we must **seriously** reduce stress as well. Stress can raise your blood pressure, which, in turn, puts great strain on your heart as well as causing possible circulatory disease. This is quite an extreme example, but it goes to show that we should all take stress seriously.

Stress and exercise

We often talk with clients who are suffering from stress. Some of the early questions we ask focus on lifestyle – especially the amount of exercise taken. Many tell us that they don't exercise at all: 'Too busy.' 'Used to, but gave it up.' 'There is little that appeals to me.' 'The gym closed down.'

In a sense, they are telling us, 'I am much too stressed out to think about exercise.' Yet exercise might be their solution.

You can learn more about the benefits of exercise in Chapter 5 of this book.

Activity Your exercise regime

- A simple question today: 'How much exercise do you take at present?'

- In view of the above, are you prepared to do more? Jot it down – we'll come back to this later.

MEASURE AND MONITOR YOUR STRESS LEVELS

How can you be sure it's stress?

> **Today you will learn ...**
>
> that stress is an important contributory factor of certain physical problems, but it may not be the whole story.

Think about any 'niggles' you have had over the last months. Many of these may have been related to stress. Stress leads to muscular tension that can cause a variety of disorders – the stress headache being the most common. Chest pain, back pain, even grinding your teeth can be a symptom of muscular reaction to stress.

Have you ever sat at dinner with someone when suddenly their stomach springs to life and they start to feel queasy and unwell? Often, when you solicitously ask what the problem is, the answer given is, 'I'm under so much stress. It's gone to my stomach. I think stress is giving me an ulcer.'

Just an excuse?

This may sound like an excuse to cover up an embarrassing moment, but it may well be partially true. A stressed stomach is probably the most common complaint after a stress headache. Your stomach lining becomes more acidic and can lead to a variety of gastric problems from simple diarrhoea to such problems as Irritable Bowel Syndrome (IBS).

Could it be an ulcer?

This is unlikely. Ulcers are more often caused by rogue bacteria. Nonetheless, the fact remains that stress can be the culprit, and all stomach complaints should be checked out for this.

Is it definitely stress?

As therapists, doctors quite often send us patients with IBS, which can successfully be sent on its way with stress management techniques.

However, in the last year we have seen two clients, referred to us for stress, only to conclude early in their treatment that this was not the right diagnosis. In each case, a second medical opinion showed them to have a medical, not psychological condition. So don't make any assumptions about the cause of your difficulties – check with your doctor first.

In the last 20 years or so there has been a growing amount of research undertaken to find links between stress and a variety of serious illnesses such as cancer, diabetes, arthritis, etc. We need to point out, however, that at the time of writing, there is no conclusive evidence that these links exist. At the same time, stress **can** contribute to illness – this is perhaps the strongest reason of all for learning how to control and/or eliminate stress for good.

TOP TIP

- Whilst stress has, in the main, a psychological basis, there is no doubt that it can be linked to a variety of physical illnesses.
- However, **always** ensure that you discuss any worries with your doctor before you make any assumptions in this regard.

Activity **Your aches and pains**

- Make a note in your diary of any aches and pains you have had recently. Considering what you have read above, write a big 'S' beside any that now sound as though they may have been caused by stress.

- Does it make you feel better, or worse, to know that? It should make you feel better, as it will be a lot easier to get rid of stress than a pulmonary embolism, for example.

MEASURE AND MONITOR YOUR STRESS LEVELS

Fight – slay the stress dragon! ...

> **Today you will learn ...**
>
> to understand how your body helps you out when your brain goes on strike.

Our bodies have evolved to react to stress, and to help us out at times when our minds freeze or become befuddled.

We need to understand something of how this has worked in our favour since time began. Then we are more able to appreciate how the 'fight or flight' trigger can sometimes give us wrong signals and messages in the 21st century.

Feelings of stress are the result of a normal bodily reaction to danger or threat in the world about us. Scientists believe that it developed in the early days of human evolution, when cave-dwellers faced many dangers in their lives. This bodily reaction, called 'automatic arousal', helped prepare the caveman and cavewoman either to fight or to run away when faced with danger. Cave-dwelling in Neanderthal times was not a recipe for a long life. With a very short average life span, the average stress trigger in those days would have been the roar of a sabre-tooth tiger.

You can see from the picture how this arousal response causes many feelings and symptoms which are similar to those which occur when you feel stressed.

When facing danger, messages pass from the brain to different parts of the body, telling it to speed up and be prepared for extra activity. This is your fight or flight response. You will not be adversely affected physically in any way from these symptoms. Your body is simply responding to a 'danger' signal from the brain, and is trying to assist you to be ready to run or fight.

◎ ➤ TOP TIP

- Physical symptoms are actually our body's way of helping us in anxious moments. It is not trying to make us sick.

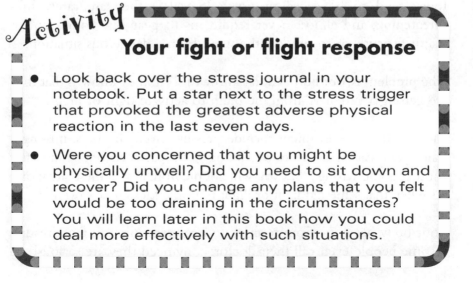

Increased sweating
– clammy hands
– feeling hot and sweaty

Increased blood pressure
– flushes
– ringing in ears
– tingling in hands

Rapid breathing
– breathlessness
– choking sensations
– dizziness/fainting
– difficulty in swallowing

Increased heart rate
– palpitations
– heart racing

Increased muscle tension
– stammering
– tightness in throat, chest, neck
– butterflies in stomach
– shaky fingers
– legs and feet like jelly

Activity

Your fight or flight response

- Look back over the stress journal in your notebook. Put a star next to the stress trigger that provoked the greatest adverse physical reaction in the last seven days.

- Were you concerned that you might be physically unwell? Did you need to sit down and recover? Did you change any plans that you felt would be too draining in the circumstances? You will learn later in this book how you could deal more effectively with such situations.

MEASURE AND MONITOR YOUR STRESS LEVELS

... Or flight – run for your life!

Features of the age-old fight or flight response that you will recognise, are:

Today you will learn ...

to understand the physiology of stress reactions.

- ◆ Your heart beats faster (your brain has worked out that you may need more blood to be sent to your muscles for fleeing or fighting).
- ◆ You breathe more rapidly to increase the air supply to your lungs.
- ◆ Your liver releases extra glucose for quick energy.
- ◆ Your pupils dilate (to help you see the enemy, or the way to safety, more clearly).

These physiological responses enabled us to deal as best as we could with the day-to-day stress triggers of the prehistoric era – large, frightening wild animals, marauding savages out to kill us, famine, fire and pestilence, to name but a few.

However, what was helpful in prehistoric times, can actually exacerbate our symptoms of stress in the modern era. If you understand this, it will no longer frighten you. The stresses we face today tend to be social or psychological – they are rarely life-threatening, and almost never require us to gear our bodies up for major fisticuffs or to run like the wind from a dangerous situation.

The problem is, our bodies don't know this! All they know is that they are getting a 'red alert' from the brain to activate fight or flight.

Modern-day stresses might include pressure from the boss, missing a train, your car breaking down, losing your passport, one thing after another going wrong – but you will not die from any of these situations. So when that same old fight or flight response kicks in, it's overkill.

Your body has gone from reacting to over-reacting. You feel dreadful – some people even call their doctor, convinced they are seriously ill or about to have a heart attack. This is a bodily error message received from a stressed-out brain.

So first, do be assured that when you have these feelings, your body is simply trying to help you – not to cause you any distress. You are physically fine!

Second, you need to retrain your mind to stop producing these erroneous and physically exhausting error messages. You can achieve this both by adjusting your thinking, and using a variety of techniques to calm your body down.

TOP TIP

- ◆ Fight or flight is a bodily response to help us survive physical danger.
- ◆ It serves us excellently in those circumstances, but can cause us to receive error messages about the scale of the problem.
- ◆ We can learn to correct these error messages, and, most importantly, even when we feel physically drained, no harm is being done to our bodies.

Activity

Begin to deal with the physical symptoms of stress

- ● Make sure that you understand the physiology of stress reactions so that you can be more aware of them when they arise.

- ● Think about what you will tell yourself next time you have worrying physical symptoms at the same time as you are feeling anxious or stressed.

MEASURE AND MONITOR YOUR STRESS LEVELS

Overcoming obstacles

Almost every time we make a decision to do something new or different – something that will give a result we feel we may get excited about – our enthusiasm for the project rises enormously.

Today you will learn ...

how to dodge all those excuses for copping out of following through!

Hopefully, you are feeling this way about conquering your stress, especially now that your knowledge and understanding have improved hugely. It is now time to embark on creating your toolbox of skills and techniques.

However, enthusiasm can wane! Remember those few pounds you vowed to lose that never actually came off? The clutter left in the attic when sorting it out became too much of a chore? Perhaps even the book you always intended to write? In any event, you get the gist. Projects we start with gusto can bite the dust if we don't find a lot of ways to prevent that happening.

So your goal for today and tomorrow is to ensure that you are organised and prepared to countermand difficulties and excuses that may come up.

What are the most common excuses you use to give yourself permission to abandon something you wish you had not embarked on in the first place?

_____

_____

_____

TOP TIP

- Don't fall at the first fence. Recognise your usual excuses and challenge them.

Your answer will enable you to plan ahead of time. Now you need to think of counter-suggestions to combat your excuses. For example:

'I'm just too busy and cannot find the time.'

- I only need to find 15 minutes a day.
- I could find that at bedtime.

'I don't really feel so stressed now. Perhaps I don't need all this effort.'

- I have suffered from stress for a long time.
- The fact that I am less stressed currently does not mean I have resolved my problems. In fact, it gives me more time and opportunity to learn these new skills for the future.

'I've tried self-help books before and they don't seem to work.'

- That does not mean this book won't work. It is action-orientated so, whatever happens, I am going to learn new skills and techniques on a daily basis.

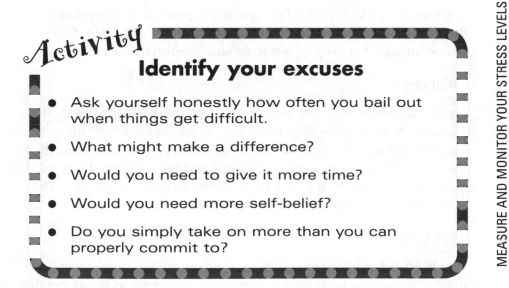

Activity

Identify your excuses

- Ask yourself honestly how often you bail out when things get difficult.
- What might make a difference?
- Would you need to give it more time?
- Would you need more self-belief?
- Do you simply take on more than you can properly commit to?

MEASURE AND MONITOR YOUR STRESS LEVELS

'Victory awaits the person who has everything in order. People call it luck. Defeat is certain for the person who has failed to take the necessary precautions. People call this bad luck.'
Roald Amundsen, Arctic explorer

How not to make excuses

Goal-setting

Make sure you have set yourself goals, but make these small and relatively easy to begin with. As mentioned in the introduction, thinking in terms of 100 days may seem daunting. So think in terms of one day, or one week, and don't look beyond that.

> **Today you will learn ...**
>
> skills to keep you going when all around you are failing.

Slow down

Alternatively, slow down. Decide to give yourself two days instead of one, a week instead of a day – even a complete break from time to time – whatever works for you. The important point with goal-setting is that you are consistent about keeping to them. If they are too difficult, change them – but keep to whatever you alternatively decide.

Uniqueness

We are all different. There may be parts of this book that seem less relevant to you personally, parts that seem tailor-made for your personal lifestyle. So increase the time you spend on the areas that resonate with you and seem meaningful and helpful. Spend less time on the others. But do at least look at all the chapters – you just never know when something may strike a chord with you unexpectedly.

Stick with it

People often hope for very quick results from stress management. But stress management takes time to learn – like learning to be an expert tennis player, you need to practise. So be patient. You may have developed your stressful habits and lifestyle over a long period of time. You may see major change in a reasonably short time – but we cannot offer overnight success.

Revisit your goals, as small successes will excite and encourage you. Re-read your list of the benefits of managing stress to inspire you. Look forward to how you would like your life to be.

⊙⤙ TOP TIP

- ◆ Be prepared. Set goals to suit you. Review them and change them so as not to pressurise yourself – but ensure that you stick to them.
- ◆ Be realistic. The fact that Rome was not built in a day did not prevent a beautiful city eventually being created.

Plan your goals

First and foremost, write down in your notebook your goals for the course. Then, take the time to write down how you plan to meet your goals.

- ● Are your goals realistic (for example, 30 minutes per day)? Would you be better to allocate less time which you would be more likely to stick to?

- ● Are you able to work on this daily? Do you need to build in breaks?

- ● How will you handle extra pressures to ensure that you don't give up?

MEASURE AND MONITOR YOUR STRESS LEVELS

Your notes

CHAPTER 3

THINKING YOUR WAY OUT OF STRESS

'Hamlet – Why, then 'tis none to you; for there is nothing either good or bad but thinking makes it so.'
William Shakespeare

Thinking styles

Today you will learn ...

that thinking-style changes can help to reduce stress more easily than lifestyle changes.

You now know a great deal about stress, and especially, your own particular stress triggers – what presses your own personal buttons and makes you want to tear your hair out or strangle someone. You should also have some idea of the levels of stress that you are attempting to cope with, as well as seeing patterns of stress, and know what makes you feel better or worse.

Hopefully, you have also learnt that stress can be reduced or eliminated, and that you won't necessarily have to change your life, and move to a tree house in a mountain retreat in Tibet in order to find inner calm and a better balanced life.

Now that you know all this, the real work starts.

You have learned the differences between pressure (which is good for you) and stress (which is bad for you). You will now be able to choose whether to run with pressure or eliminate stress.

Remember, it is not necessarily the events in our lives which cause stress but rather:

- **Our perceptions of those events** – do we see failure to land the job that we want, get the man we like or do well in an exam (for examples) as a complete catastrophe from which it will be hard to recover, or more reasonably, as a disappointment from which we can learn and move on from?
- **Our default thinking style** – seeing the glass as 'half empty or half full'. This refers to our default thinking style. In other words, are we optimistically inclined, or pessimistically inclined? You may already have an awareness of this. A good test is to think of half a dozen friends, and then decide if they are optimists or pessimists. What is it that makes them seem this way to you? What can you learn from this?
- **Our attitudes** – we are often scarcely aware of these, as we have usually honed them over many years. They may be negative – 'shop assistants never care about their customers', 'people who believe' in horoscopes are all idiots', or they may be optimistic – 'people are generally very helpful', 'I can appreciate others' points of view, even if I disagree with them'.

The great news is that working on changing your thinking can be a lot easier than making drastic changes in your lifestyle.

◎─✎ TOP TIP

- How you feel is more dependent on how you think about what happens than on what actually happens.

Activity ■■■■■■■■■■■■■ **Your default thinking style**

- Based on the above, what would you say is your default thinking style?

THINKING YOUR WAY OUT OF STRESS

Are you keeping up? Do you need some help? If you've not already subscribed, why not try the daily text messaging service for extra encouragement and support. Just text 'Mellow 21' to 80881 now.

Each set of messages costs £1.50. Please see page xii for full terms and conditions.

The ABC model

American psychologist Dr Albert Ellis achieved fame in the 1960s for his innovative work in the area of thoughts and perceptions. He developed his model

> **Today you will learn ...**
>
> about A, B, C thinking.

(Rational Emotive Behaviour Therapy) from the original work of Eastern philosophers. You may be familiar with Epictetus' famous pronouncement, 'People are disturbed not by things, but by the views that they take of them.'

A,B,C

We call this the ABC model of stress.

A = The **A**ctivating event or situation.
    For example, your boss hauls you over the coals for a poor piece of work.
C = The **C**onsequences.
    You feel depressed (emotional reaction), your stomach churns (physiological reaction), you worry (cognitive – 'thinking' – reaction) and end up drowning your sorrows in the pub (behavioural reaction).

TOP TIP

- You can reduce stress more easily by changing your thinking about your life than by actually changing your life.
- Events, in themselves, are not the stress triggers – but your beliefs about those events could make you extremely stressed.

THINKING YOUR WAY OUT OF STRESS

Does it make sense to you that the Cs (the consequences) were caused by the A (the event)?

Yes ☐   No ☐

If you ticked 'No', why?

_____

_____

_____

The correct answer is 'No'.
It is the B that is responsible for the C, not the A.

B stands for **B**eliefs (about the event).

Your boss criticising you was not responsible for any of the Consequences of this Activating event. Your **Beliefs** about the event were the cause. These were your 'thinking' reactions, which might have been 'I'll get the sack for this.' 'I'm hopeless at my job.' 'It's all downhill from here on,' etc.

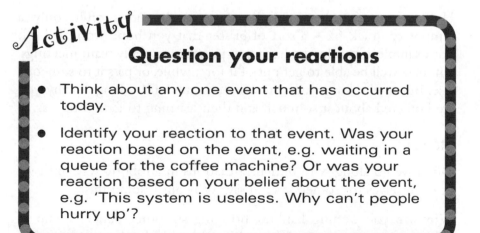

Activity

Question your reactions

- Think about any one event that has occurred today.

- Identify your reaction to that event. Was your reaction based on the event, e.g. waiting in a queue for the coffee machine? Or was your reaction based on your belief about the event, e.g. 'This system is useless. Why can't people hurry up'?

THINKING YOUR WAY OUT OF STRESS

Understanding your 'A's

The activating event

Let's take a look at events. We often cannot change what happens to us. Our lives have many immovable elements and responsibilities, and we need to learn to deal with these in a less stressful way.

> **Today you will learn ...**
>
> about removing stressors.

However, sometimes we can change things.

What we are referring to here is **removing stressors**. Where we can, we should. So take a moment to think about the ways in which you can do this.

Avoidance

It doesn't make sense to put yourself into situations that you know are going to tense you right up and stress you right out. If you're frightened of dogs, you can steer clear of dogs. If you don't like heights, the Eiffel Tower is not for you. If you're not good at last-minute rushes, you can start your projects earlier on.

However, one weakness of avoidance is that it is often only a temporary quick-fix – a sort of plaster that you hope won't fall off. For example, if you loathe having to present at weekly team meetings, you may well be able to get out of it for a while, or pass it to someone else. But in the long run, you will be better off looking at why you are bothered about it so much and then learning to face your fear.

Stopping

Often we go along with difficult situations in a robotic way, until we hear ourselves (or someone else) say, 'Why am I doing this?'

Why **are** you ironing hankies, bringing six other people a cup of coffee every time you get one, putting up with the guy who sits next to you at lunch each day and drones on and on about his problems?

Stop doing it!

Getting help

Do you get in to work each day and have to hit the coffee machine six times to get it to make you that 'kick start' cuppa that you need? Start to think creatively – why not bring in a kettle and some coffee sachets? Why not call in at a coffee shop on the way in?

We all know many people who constantly complain about their mobile phone that plays up, the uncomfortable chair that they sit in, the way their desk faces a poor outlook or the lighting is not to their liking.

The answer is – change it!

Where you can add resources that will make your life easier, calmer and less bothersome, this is what you should do.

Re-thinking

Like avoidance, re-thinking involves being aware that you don't need to put up with a stressful situation. Unlike avoidance, you use a certain amount of creative thinking instead of simply dodging the issue. 'Instead of doing something this way, could I perhaps do it that way?'

Change your reactions

- Look back over the last week. Think of one stressful situation where you could use avoidance, one where you could actually just 'stop it', one where you might change things, and one where you might re-think the situation.

- Write these down with the date next to them.

- In about a week's time, check which of these situations you are actually reacting differently to now.

THINKING YOUR WAY OUT OF STRESS

Challenging your 'A's

> **Today you will learn ...**
>
> to begin to question stress-inducing thinking.

Think of half a dozen situations right now that you get stressed about on a day-to-day basis. Then stop and think for a moment about any change you could make to make life easier.

Here are some suggestions.

Stressful event	Adjustment(s) I could make
Getting the children ready on time for school in the mornings is hugely stressful.	◆ We could all get up earlier. ◆ I could get up before the children. ◆ We could get stuff ready the previous evening. ◆ I can let others take more responsibility for ensuring that they're ready. If they're not, they're not. They'll learn!
The traffic on your way to work gets worse and worse. By the time you arrive now, you have smoke coming out of your ears from frustration.	◆ I could leave earlier and take the longer but less traffic-ridden route. ◆ I could look at public transport – at least I could read on the train. ◆ I could invest in some audiotapes of books I want to read and never have time.

THINKING YOUR WAY OUT OF STRESS

These examples may be way off the mark for you, but will give you the idea.

We are not talking about major life changes (that comes later!) This is simply about looking at everyday stressors that you could possibly make changes to – but have not thought about yet.

 TOP TIP

- Only change things that you get really stressed about. A lot of what goes on is more to do with your attitude, and you can change that, too.

Activity **Beat your stressors**

- Now take your notebook and write down some ideas of your own. Then brainstorm possible adjustments and think how they might work for you.

- This exercise will encourage you think more creatively about stressors, rather than just putting up with them.

THINKING YOUR WAY OUT OF STRESS

51

Facts or beliefs?

It doesn't matter how strongly or fervently you believe something – that doesn't necessarily make it true!

One of the difficulties that many of us have is in appreciating the difference between a belief and a fact. Here are some examples.

Today you will learn ...

the difference between facts and beliefs, and why this is so important.

- I can't sew.
- Meat is bad for you.
- Driving at night is more dangerous than driving in the daytime.
- Babies need to be fed every four hours to ensure they develop a routine.
- The Government is useless.
- Flying is really dangerous.
- I could earn a lot more money working for XYZ Co.

> How many of the above statements do you think are beliefs? ☐
> And how many do you think are facts? ☐
> ★

How easy was it to tell the difference?

People tend – especially when under stress – to operate on the principle that a belief is a fact. This is problematic when trying to decide on the meaning of an event, since, whilst beliefs can be challenged, facts are facts and, therefore, unchallengeable.

Now test out your own stress-inducing beliefs.

Do you recognise any of the following? Circle the strength of your belief, where 'S' represents strongly, 'M' represents moderately and 'W' represents weakly. For Question 25, note down any additional beliefs you hold that cause you further stress.

1	S	M	W	Events should go smoothly.
2	S	M	W	Work must be exciting and stimulating.
3	S	M	W	If I lost my job, it would be awful.
4	S	M	W	If I lost my job, I could not bear it.
5	S	M	W	My job is one of the most important things to me.
6	S	M	W	I must perform well at all important tasks.
7	S	M	W	My work should be recognised by others.
8	S	M	W	I am indispensable at work.
9	S	M	W	I must enjoy myself whatever I am doing.
10	S	M	W	I must not get bored.
11	S	M	W	I should not encounter problems.
12	S	M	W	I should have the solitude I deserve.
13	S	M	W	I must escape from responsibilities and demands.
14	S	M	W	I should be treated fairly.
15	S	M	W	I should be treated as special.
16	S	M	W	I should be in control of all significant situations.
17	S	M	W	Others should respect me.
18	S	M	W	I should get on well with my friends and family.
19	S	M	W	My children should do well in life.
20	S	M	W	If things went badly, it would be awful.
21	S	M	W	If things went badly, I could not stand it.
22	S	M	W	Things never work out well for me.
23	S	M	W	If things go wrong, those responsible are stupid, useless, idiots or failures.
24	S	M	W	If I fail at a task, that proves I'm a failure or useless.
25	S	M	W	Additional beliefs _____

Now, count up how many 'S's you found. What does this tell you? You know the answer, of course – the beliefs you hold are a major cause of your stress.

Activity Identify your beliefs

- In your notebook, write down six beliefs that you hold strongly. For example,
  - It was right to ban fox-hunting.
  - Success in life is dependent upon hard work.

- Now imagine someone tells you that you are wrong to think this way. Give a rating of between 0 (= That's fine, I can see their point of view) and 10 (= They are so wrong!) to each one. Add up your total score. The higher it is, the more prone you are to the type of rigid thinking that can induce stress.

THINKING YOUR WAY OUT OF STRESS

* In fact, they are all beliefs.

'People are disturbed not by things but the views which they take of them.' Epictetus, stoic philosopher

Why should you change your beliefs?

Today you will learn ...

how to begin to think more flexibly – and thus, less stressfully.

Of course you do not have to change your beliefs. However, you will by now have realised that some of your beliefs may be stress-inducing and self-defeating. So it makes sense to adjust those which are not helping you. Many of your beliefs will be beneficial – you need to look only at those which cause you stress.

Remember, beliefs are not necessarily facts. Beliefs are thoughts that you may have had for a while, based on certain assumptions, but they really are open to question and debate.

The trick is to debate them – with yourself!

Look again at the beliefs indicator test you did yesterday. First of all, get a pen and strike through each of the following words each time it appears.

should   must   never   stand   bear   awful

Leaves a lot of gaps, doesn't it?

Learning to be less rigid in your thinking

Now you need to replace each of these words with a 'softer' word, phrase or sentence. For example, change 'Events should go smoothly' to 'It would be nice if events usually went smoothly'. Work through the rest of the gaps, making similar replacements.

Next, you need to start challenging some of these beliefs. To begin with, you will need to do this in your notebook. Challenge the six beliefs you noted down yesterday.

Over time, you will come to internalise the process.

Belief: 'I should be treated fairly.'

Challenges: 'Whilst it is great to be treated fairly, realistically we sometimes get a bum deal.'
'I probably get treated fairly more often than not.'
'Everyone has their own idea of what fair treatment is.'

For each belief, you should be able to come up with at least two or three alternatives. You don't have to believe them totally yet – just start to stretch your thinking.

TOP TIP

- ♦ Beliefs are not facts, and can be wrong.
- ♦ By ridding our thinking of extreme wording, and replacing it with softer wording, we actually disturb ourselves less.
- ♦ Challenging stress-inducing beliefs can help us to see situations and events in a more relaxed way.

Activity
Challenging your beliefs

- • Read the challenges you have come up with at least three times.

- • Get used to thinking them, even if you don't believe them.

THINKING YOUR WAY OUT OF STRESS

How 'B's affect 'C's

CASE STUDY

James plays football on Sunday mornings. Every Sunday at 9 am sharp, he gets the bus to the football ground to join his mates for a friendly game. They usually play another local team, and occasionally play in League games.

One weekend, James had a big night out on the Saturday evening. He also forgot to set his alarm clock. He woke up on Sunday morning at 9.15 am. James leapt out of bed in shock, and then he thought, 'This is hopeless. I'll never get there in time now. Everyone will be so cross. In fact, I'll probably get dropped from the team, since I haven't been playing that well recently. They'll ask Rob instead now.' As James thought these ideas, he began to feel really upset. He lay back on the bed, depressed – he even resolved to resign from the team before he got pushed. He closed his eyes and fell back to sleep.

Later in the day, the phone rang. It was one of his team-mates. 'Hi James – where did you get to this morning?' James sighed, 'Oh, I overslept. It was just all too late – I knew Rob would replace me. I expect he played really well?' 'You idiot, James!' came the reply, 'You should just have come along in any event. Three members of the opposition failed to turn up, and one of our lot got badly injured in the first five minutes, so the whole game was held up until 11 am, and we really missed you.'

Read through today's case study. Now ask yourself:

Today you will learn ...

how negative beliefs can promote stressful consequences.

◆ Did James miss a great game of football because of his 'A' (getting up late)?
◆ Or was it because of his 'B' (his beliefs about how awful this was)?
◆ What were the 'C' (consequences) to James of this?

The moral is, if you want to change your 'C's and you can't change your 'A's, you need to change your 'B's.

We have now looked at 'A's, 'B's and 'C's on their own. Tomorrow we are going to bring the whole thing together, and throw in 'D's and 'E's.

TOP TIP

◆ A–C thinking allows us to blame external events or other people for our stress.
◆ B–C thinking helps us to take responsibility for our stress. This is good news, because it means we can work on changing things.

Activity Alternative 'B's

● Read through James' story again. Get your notebook and jot down some alternative 'B's that would have changed the consequences of that day for him.

● Attempt to come up with at least two or three alternatives.

THINKING YOUR WAY OUT OF STRESS

'After a storm comes a calm.'
Mathew Henry, *Commentaries, Acts ix*

'D's and 'E's – what are they?

'D' stands for '**D**isputing belief'.

'E' stands for '**E**nergising outcome'.

> **Today you will learn ...**
>
> how negative beliefs can promote stressful consequences.

Whilst an energising outcome cannot always be the answer to your prayers, it will – as the name implies – make things a great deal better than the negative consequences of the negative belief.

Chart it

On the opposite page is a chart that explains this clearly. We have given a simple example to get you started.

TOP TIP

- 'D's and 'E's are an important part of your total thinking processes.
- They are important as they help you to dispute your initial thinking, which will, hopefully, give you a better outcome.

Activity
A–E chart

- Fill in two or three other stressful situations (either on-going, or one-offs).

- Follow through with the beliefs and consequences – and then add your D and E.

Challenging your thoughts

A Adversity	B Negative Belief	C Negative Consequence	D Disputing belief	E Energising outcome
Turned down for job interview several times.	'I'm not good enough.' 'I'll never get a job.'	Feel depressed. Lose confidence. Stop bothering.	'Jobs are hard to come by for everyone. It's not personal. I'll have another go as I do have lots to offer.'	Have another go at getting an interview. Increases confidence, eventually will get job offer.

THINKING YOUR WAY OUT OF STRESS

'The one person whom it is most necessary to reform is yourself.'
Ralph Waldo Emerson

But it's not that easy ...

From what we have done so far, you can see that the way you think has an important effect on the way you feel and what you

> **Today you will learn ...**
>
> to capture your negative thoughts.

are able to do. Pessimistic, negative thoughts such as 'I can't cope', or 'I feel terrible' make you feel more anxious and unhappy and can themselves be a major cause of your stress.

This is negative B–C thinking, and you are now learning to dispute and challenge these thoughts and beliefs.

However, it is one thing to understand all this in theory, but quite another to be able to easily make the necessary changes.

Clients often tell us of their negative beliefs: 'They are always there. I don't know where they come from. I can't do anything about them.'

This is one of the major problems people find in getting rid of stressful, depressive thoughts and ruminations. They seem to invade our brains and we just don't know where they came from! Sometimes they are called 'pop-up' thoughts.

Be aware of negative thoughts

Just becoming aware of these negative thoughts can help you to understand why you are worried by them, and is the initial step towards reducing negative emotions and learning to think in a more helpful, constructive way. To help you become more aware of these thoughts, you need to know a little more about what negative thoughts 'look like'.

TOP TIP

- Learning to identify the negative thoughts is a first good step towards changing your thinking.

THINKING YOUR WAY OUT OF STRESS

The following list suggests characteristics that negative thoughts have in common:

◆ They spring to mind without any effort from you.
◆ They are easy to believe.
◆ They are often not true.
◆ They can be difficult to stop.
◆ They are unhelpful.
◆ They keep you anxious and make it difficult to change.

These negative thoughts may be difficult to spot to start with – you are probably not always aware that you have them. The first step is to learn to recognise them. This is where some of the previous work you have done now comes in. You have started to challenge beliefs where you may not previously have considered any alternatives. You have done an exercise where you start to consider new 'D's.

It really doesn't matter if you don't believe your new 'D's yet. What you are doing is learning to think more broadly and, often, more optimistically. In time, your negative automatic thoughts will stop being the first ideas that come into your head. More hopeful and helpful thinking will become the norm.

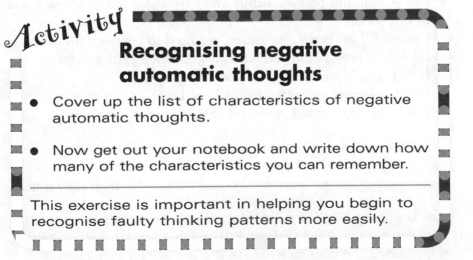

Activity

Recognising negative automatic thoughts

● Cover up the list of characteristics of negative automatic thoughts.

● Now get out your notebook and write down how many of the characteristics you can remember.

This exercise is important in helping you begin to recognise faulty thinking patterns more easily.

Replacing your 'B's

You are beginning to learn that challenging your negative thoughts in a more helpful, realistic way can help you to cope with your worries. However, it can still be hard to think of coping thoughts or statements (your 'D's) which will help you respond to your own particular negative thoughts.

> **Today you will learn ...**
>
> some ideas for more helpful thoughts.

Here is a list of coping statements which may give you some ideas. Read through it and think about which of these might apply to you and help you to deal with your worries in a more positive and constructive way.

Coping statements

- I'm going to face this problem/situation so that I can practise coping better.
- It's unlikely that it will work completely, but the important issue is to practise and build up my confidence.
- I know that worry makes me feel worse. I know my feelings can be controlled.
- I've been in this position before and have come out of it alive / still in one piece.
- I know I'll get better the more I get used to coping with stress.
- I'll feel so proud of myself when I feel myself getting calmer.
- It feels good learning how to control stressful feelings.
- I'm deliberately going to change how I feel.
- I'm living proof that I can stand almost everything.

The above are just examples to get you started. Now think up at least six coping statements of your own that are relevant to your particular problems. You can use your notebook, or fill in the chart shown here.

The key to thinking in a more balanced way is to keep practising. Every time you become aware of negative thoughts going through your mind, stop yourself and think of some realistic and helpful alternatives.

THINKING YOUR WAY OUT OF STRESS

My coping statements

1 _____
2 _____
3 _____
4 _____
5 _____
6 _____

When preparing to go into a situation which you know will be extremely stressful, think beforehand about what coping skills you will use (e.g. perhaps a breathing exercise – see the next chapter) and how you will challenge any negative thoughts before, during and afterwards.

When you suspect that your thoughts are negative or unrealistic, ask yourself:

◆ Is this really true?
◆ Is there another way of looking at this?
◆ What was I afraid might be going to happen?
◆ What was happening, or going through my mind, just before I began feeling this way?
◆ Am I recalling any past incidences where things turned out poorly?

TOP TIP

◆ Having a 'stock' of coping statements can help you deal more effectively with stressful periods.
◆ Preparing ahead of time, when you know you are going into a stressful situation, can make a huge difference.

Activity
Coping

● Go to the back of your notebook and start a 'Coping statements' page. Write down at least a dozen right now.

● Add to this list regularly and read them regularly.

THINKING YOUR WAY OUT OF STRESS

A reminder – write it down!

One of the most useful things you can do when training yourself in stress-management is to continually challenge your negative beliefs. The chart from Day 27 is a good way of doing this.

> **Today you will learn ...**
>
> writing thoughts down will help you to distinguish between negative thoughts and rational thoughts.

This type of chart is often called a 'thought record', since although you are recording what has happened, the main focus is on what you **thought** about what happened.

The more you practise filling in a thought record, the easier it becomes to spot these thoughts, and to understand the effect they have on how you feel.

It may be quite a new idea, to remember what you were thinking when you were worried or feeling low, and it may take some practice before you get the hang of it. Next time you find yourself becoming tense or worried, as soon as you can, sit down and fill in your thought record. You can describe the physical sensations you experienced as well as the thoughts that went through your head at the time.

Once you are familiar with identifying negative thoughts, you can keep track of them and examine how unrealistic or unhelpful they are, and whether they are useful to you. As your learned on Day 27, if they are unrealistic or unhelpful you can challenge them with what we call a disputing belief. You will now be becoming familiar with this – your 'D' – the reply that you make to these thoughts, based on firm evidence. Studies have shown that doing this can improve your mood and make you feel more in control of your situation and your life.

Just to check that you have understood what you have read so far, jot down below what you consider, in the context of the work we are doing, these alphabet letters to stand for:

A _____

B _____

C _____

D _____

E _____

TOP TIP

◆ Simply having an awareness of negative thinking (rather than assuming that it is rational thinking!) can help us feel better.

◆ The more often you jot these thoughts down, the easier they will become to spot – and then dispute.

Activity Write it down

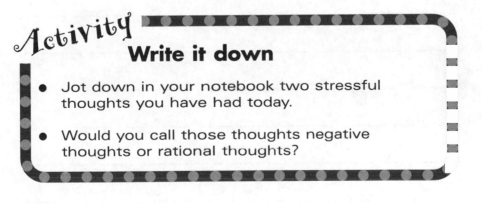

● Jot down in your notebook two stressful thoughts you have had today.

● Would you call those thoughts negative thoughts or rational thoughts?

THINKING YOUR WAY OUT OF STRESS

Your notes

CHAPTER 4

TRACK DOWN
YOUR PERSONAL
STRESS SOURCE

Are you keeping up? Do you need some help? If you've not already subscribed, why not try the daily text messaging service for extra encouragement and support. Just text 'Mellow 31' to 80881 now.

Each set of messages costs £1.50. Please see page xii for full terms and conditions.

'Remember to keep a calm mind in difficulties.' Horace

Tracking down stress triggers

Whilst challenging our negative thinking and beliefs is one of the most important tools in defeating stress, it is not always a simple task. We sometimes hear people saying, 'Oh, that's all very well, but it never works for me.'

> **Today you will learn ...**
>
> about mistakes we can make when using thought-challenging to reduce stress.

If something isn't working, it is easy to give up trying. However, it may not be working for a reason – and that can be corrected.

Sometimes people find that 'thought-challenging' has no helpful effect because they are challenging the wrong thought.

In order to properly challenge our negative thoughts and beliefs, we need to be sure we are accurately working out just what the correct negative thought – the stress trigger – is. It's a bit like detective work.

TRACK DOWN YOUR PERSONAL STRESS SOURCE

For example, imagine you feel so stressed out that you need to sit down and breathe deeply in order to recover. Then you ask yourself what might have caused that, and the thought that comes into your mind is, 'I wasn't sure what to cook for dinner tonight.'

Really? Not knowing what to cook for dinner tonight caused you to feel so stressed and upset that you had to sit down? More likely you need to dig a little deeper to access what was really bothering you, in order to deal with the problem.

In this case, for instance, further probing may have uncovered that the reason you were so stressed is that your relationship had been on very shaky ground recently. Amongst other things, your partner had been very critical of your cooking, and the previous evening there had been a big row over the fact that you should have known he didn't like sausages.

TOP TIP

♦ When thought-challenging doesn't seem to help lift your mood, you may be challenging the wrong thought.

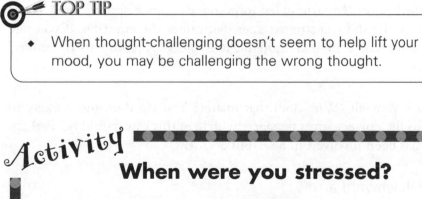

Activity When were you stressed?

● Have you felt stressed in the last week, without being able to pinpoint quite why?

● Write down the times that you felt this way, where you were, and what you were doing.

TRACK DOWN YOUR PERSONAL STRESS SOURCE

Unearthing the real problem

> **Today you will learn ...**
>
> some skills for working out
> what's really going on.

One of the biggest problems for people who feel stressed out on a chronic, on-going basis is that of pin-pointing exactly what the problem is.

Here are some skills that you can use when 'digging around' to discover what thoughts or beliefs are really stressing you out.

Rate it

This means rating your stress levels on the one hand, and the importance of your thought on the other, and seeing whether there is a 'match'.

For example, if your mood rating is 'Stress (90%)', a negative thought on the lines of, 'My friend has forgotten our lunch appointment' is not going to be the real stress trigger that causes the emotion. If you rate the importance of that thought, it is probably going to be around 20–30%.

So ask yourself, 'Why does that matter?' You are then more likely to get to the correct stress trigger – which, in this case, could be 'Perhaps she has been involved in a serious accident.'

The downward arrow

This is an excellent skill for getting to the bottom of your stresses. You can use it in a variety of situations – and with others as well as yourself. It works like this.

You feel dreadfully stressed and your head is aching. Why is this? Your first thought is:

'I can't seem to get on with the work I need to do for
this presentation.'

Ask yourself : 'Why does that matter?'
↓

Answer: 'If the presentation doesn't go well, we may lose
the client.'

Ask yourself : 'Why does that matter?'
↓

Answer: 'If we lose the client our department won't
meet its sales targets'.

Ask yourself : 'Why does that matter?'
↓

Answer: 'I'll be held responsible and I may even lose my
job.'

You can ask yourself another question instead: 'What is the personal
meaning to me if this does or doesn't occur?'

⊙ TOP TIP

- Before you can start challenging your negative thinking,
  you need to be sure that you know exactly what is really
  in your mind that is causing the stress.
- Techniques like the downward arrow can help you to do
  this – but don't use it if you are feeling depressed.

Activity
Why were you stressed?

- Practise using the downward arrow with the
  stressful occasions you noted yesterday.

- See what you discover about the stress triggers
  that are **really** bothering you.

TRACK DOWN YOUR PERSONAL STRESS SOURCE

Do emotions cause stress – or vice versa?

We've spent some time looking at thoughts, and how they can affect us. Our reaction to stress, however, isn't just made up of thoughts – it consists of feelings too. It can sometimes seem a very

physical feeling ('I'm so stressed I'm exhausted'), or sometimes it can seem to be a very emotional feeling ('I'm so stressed I could cry').

We learned in earlier chapters how negative thinking can cause negative outcomes, and the emotional outcome can be quite powerful. So you can appreciate how negative beliefs can lead to negative emotions.

For example, if Paul feels anxious about getting a poor work appraisal and has decided that this means he'll be first on the redundancy list, then the stress trigger is his negative belief ('I'll be first on the redundancy list'). That, in turn, triggers his feelings of anxiety which cause him to get quite stressed out about the situation. His negative appraisal of the situation is what is making Paul feel anxious.

Equally, however, negative emotions can trigger negative beliefs which trigger further negative emotions. Read the following example.

CASE STUDY

Jenny was asked, at the end of an already long, hard day, to work late in order to finish an important project within an unreasonably short time frame. She started feeling very anxious about reaching the deadline. Then she became aware of her physical symptoms of anxiety such as her heart beating rapidly. She started to wonder 'Am I OK? Am I seriously ill?' She literally became anxious about her anxiety! Feeling so stressed out, Jenny found it hard to focus on her work.

TRACK DOWN YOUR PERSONAL STRESS SOURCE

> The negative emotion of anxiety associated with meeting deadlines triggered physical symptoms such as a rapid heartbeat about which Jenny then had worrying pessimistic thoughts – triggering more anxiety.

As you saw in the first chapter of this book, stress can be caused by a variety of different moods or emotions, and it is important to learn how to identify these. For example, you might feel tired all the time, but fail to realise that this is because you are depressed.

So recognising moods, and understanding how they can affect our thinking just as much as our thinking can affect our moods, is another important aspect of learning to conquer stress.

TOP TIP

- Our emotions drive our thinking just as powerfully as our thinking drives our emotions.
- It is therefore very important for us to be able to identify our emotions.

Activity
Negative thinking and negative emotions

- Can you think of an example, in the past week or two, when you have allowed negative emotions to turn into negative thinking? Jot it down.

- Now find an example of negative thinking that let to a negative emotion. Jot that down as well.

- What do you learn from this?

TRACK DOWN YOUR PERSONAL STRESS SOURCE

Identifying stressful emotions

> **Today you will learn ...**
>
> how to recognise negative
> emotions more easily.

It can sometimes be difficult specifically to identify what you are thinking. This can apply to emotions as well, so here are some suggestions of a variety of moods that you might feel in a day.

> anxious   scared   shy   panicky   insecure   sad   hurt   depressed
> disappointed   empty   angry   irritated   frustrated   appalled   embarrassed
> humiliated   repulsed   sick   nauseous   guilty   ashamed   jealous   envious
> shocked   surprised   happy   excited   content   proud   concerned

Now do the following exercises.

1 Write down any further suggestions you have to add to this list.

_____   _____   _____

_____   _____   _____

2 Take a highlighter pen and score through any of the above moods you have been particularly aware of in the past month.

If you have a problem identifying emotions, being aware of bodily changes may help you – stomach churning or palpitations can signal high anxiety or panic, heaviness throughout your body can signal depression, for example.

Complete the chart using the three physical changes that have cropped up most frequently – also record the situation in which you felt these emotions. Can you recall what you were thinking on any of the occasions that these moods cropped up?

An important point here is that there should be a 'match' between the intensity of the thought and the intensity of the emotion. We have worked on this already (Day 32). Now you need to make this a habit.

TRACK DOWN YOUR PERSONAL STRESS SOURCE

	What was the situation?	What was I thinking?	Negative emotion
1			
2			
3			

If there is no match, use some of the skills you have learnt to ensure that you get one.

You will hopefully now have an increased ability to recognise emotions that may be causing stress, as well as more understanding of how negative thoughts can cause negative emotions.

At the end of the day, we come back to the same principle:

Thoughts drive **emotions** and **emotions** drive **thinking**.

If we can replace our negative, unhelpful thoughts and beliefs with those that are more constructive, we will also feel a great deal better emotionally.

TOP TIP

- ◆ Understanding this statement connecting thoughts and emotions will help you become much more able to control how you feel.
- ◆ Practise being aware of your emotions, as well as your thoughts. If there is a mismatch you are not addressing the problem.

Activity

Identify your thoughts and emotions

- ● Make sure that you have filled in the thoughts/feelings box.
- ● Continue to have a real awareness of feelings in relation to thoughts and situations.

TRACK DOWN YOUR PERSONAL STRESS SOURCE

Thinking errors

We tend to assume that all our thinking is rational and correct. In a good frame of mind it may be. But when we are feeling stressed or anxious, our thinking can become negative and distorted without our realising that this is happening.

> **Today you will learn ...**
>
> to begin to identify thinking errors that can cause your stress to rise.

The problem here is that, once we start making thinking errors, we tend to 'stick with them'. They become assumptions and beliefs that we retain unless we make an effort to recognise them and change them.

Psychologists have identified a series of common thinking errors that we are all liable to make from time to time. Today and tomorrow you will look at these and identify those that apply to you.

In the exercise below place a tick beside those that have a familiar ring. These are the thinking errors that you are making often – engrave them on your heart so that you are really aware of them! These errors are especially likely to happen when you are tired or stressed.

Copy into your notebook the particular thinking errors that you make. Check back regularly to remind yourself to stop using them.

Here are the first eight.

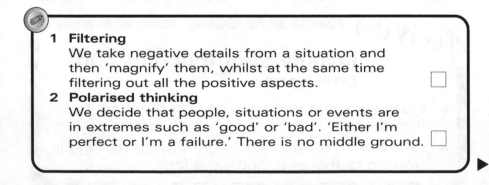

1 **Filtering**
   We take negative details from a situation and then 'magnify' them, whilst at the same time filtering out all the positive aspects. ☐

2 **Polarised thinking**
   We decide that people, situations or events are in extremes such as 'good' or 'bad'. 'Either I'm perfect or I'm a failure.' There is no middle ground. ☐

3 **Over-generalisation**
   We come to a general conclusion based on a single incident or piece of evidence. If something bad happens once, such as arriving late, we expect it to happen over and over again. ☐

4 **Mind reading**
   Without their saying so, we 'know' what people are thinking and why they act the way their do. In particular, we are able to divine how people are feeling towards us. ☐

5 **Catastrophising**
   We expect disaster. We notice or hear about a problem, and start on 'what if's': 'What if tragedy strikes?' 'What if it happens to me?' ☐

6 **Personalisation**
   We think that everything people do or say is some kind of reaction to us. We also compare ourselves to others, attempting to determine who's smarter, better looking, etc. ☐

7 **Control fallacies**
   If we feel externally controlled, we see ourselves as helpless, as victims of fate. The fallacy of internal control is that you feel responsible for the pain and happiness of everyone around you. ☐

8 **Fallacy of fairness**
   We feel resentful because we think we know what's fair, but other people won't agree with us. ☐

Activity

What are your common thinking errors? Part 1

● Pick three stressful situations in the recent past which have triggered negative thinking. Write them down. Now see if you can match those thoughts to any of the above thinking errors.

● Once you have done that, 're-think' the situation in a more rational way and write down these thoughts.

TRACK DOWN YOUR PERSONAL STRESS SOURCE

More thinking errors

Here are some more common thinking errors. Again, tick those in the list below that apply to you.

> **Today you will learn ...**
>
> to continue to identify thinking errors that can cause your stress to rise.

1 Blaming
We hold other people, organisations or even the universe responsible for our problems. ☐

2 'Shoulds', 'musts'
We have a long list of inflexible, rigid rules about how we, and other people, should or must act. People who break our rules anger us, and we feel guilty if we break our own rules. ☐

3 Emotional reasoning
We believe that what we feel must be true. If we feel stupid and boring, then we must be stupid and boring. If we feel angry at work then our boss must have treated us unfairly. ☐

4 Fallacy of change
We expect other people to change to suit us if we just pressure or cajole them enough. We attempt to change people in this way when we believe our hopes for happiness depend entirely on their behaving differently. ☐

5 Globalising
We generalise one or two negative opinions into a negative global judgement: 'I've failed my exam therefore I'm a total failure.' ☐

6 'Being right'
We continually put ourselves on trial to prove that our opinions and actions are correct. Being wrong is unthinkable and we will go to any lengths to demonstrate our 'rightness'. ☐

◄ TRACK DOWN YOUR PERSONAL STRESS SOURCE

▶

7 'Heaven's reward' fallacy
We expect all our sacrifice and denial to pay off, as if someone is keeping the score. We then feel bitter when we are not recognised and rewarded for the sacrifices we have made.

Looking back over all 15 thinking errors, how many did you tick in total?

Checking out possible thinking errors is another excellent skill to add to your toolbox of skills for closely examining your thinking. Make sure that you use it regularly.

I'm right, I'm right!

TOP TIP

◆ You need to recognise your thinking errors in order to change them.

What are your common thinking errors? Part 2

● Again, pick three stressful situations in the recent past which have triggered negative thinking. Write them down in your notebook. Now see if you can match those thoughts to any of today's thinking errors.

● Once you have done that, 're-think' the situation in a more rational way and write down these thoughts.

TRACK DOWN YOUR PERSONAL STRESS SOURCE

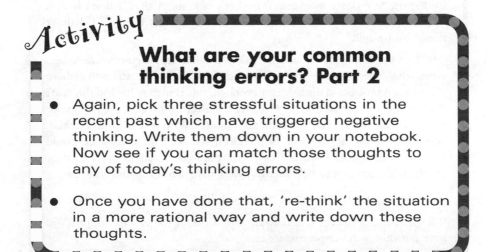

So where's the evidence?

One of the problems people have with challenging negative thinking, and replacing a negative thought with an idea that is more balanced and helpful, is that the inclination is still to believe the negative thought. Read through this typical scenario.

> **Today you will learn ...**
>
> to 'play detective' to check out your thinking.

CASE STUDY

Tom was very stressed at work and was really beginning to feel swamped and unable to cope. When he mentioned this to a colleague, Jim, his advice was to talk to his boss and explain the position. Tom said that he couldn't do this, as he was sure that his boss thought he wasn't up to the job and was looking to find a reason to get rid of him.

Tom felt more stressed than ever. Not only was he totally swamped with work that he felt he could not possibly complete on time, but now he had the worry that he might lose his job if he didn't. The extra stress caused his work-rate to slow and more mistakes to appear.

When Jim popped his head round Tom's door he could see that Tom was in despair. 'Stop for a moment, Tom. Let's talk about this.' 'I don't have a moment' said Tom, 'I'm so behind already and I'll get the sack if I don't finish this tonight.'

'Hold on there,' said Jim. 'Can I just ask you what happened two weeks ago when the Sales Awards were announced? Can I just ask you whose presentation brought in the biggest new client our company has had this year? And would you please tell me who has been recommended for the Senior Sales position when Peter retires in six months? Who is that?' Tom blushed. 'Well, me, I guess,' he said sheepishly. 'And if you were your manager, would you give someone like that the sack, or would you listen seriously to their problems and attempt to help them?' 'Well, the latter, I suppose,' said Tom.

'OK, then. What are your plans now?' said Jim.

'I'll speak to my manager,' said Tom, with a rueful smile. 'Thanks, Jim. You have put things in perspective for me.'

Negative thoughts can be very hard to shift. It may take a great deal of practice to replace pessimistic beliefs with more constructive ones. A very helpful tool – thought by many to be the most important 'thought shifter' around – is to ask a simple question: 'If this is really so, where's the evidence?'

Here is what we mean by 'looking for evidence'. Tom's thinking had become so negatively skewed that he was discounting abundant evidence that his thinking was likely to be incorrect. Once he was forced to look for evidence to back up his thinking, he could find little – but there was a great deal to show that his thinking was incorrect.

TOP TIP

- ◆ 'Where's the evidence?' is one of the most important questions you will ever ask yourself to counteract pessimistic thinking.
- ◆ Never just assume that your pessimistic thinking is correct. Always look for evidence to back it up – you may get a pleasant surprise when there is less than you think!

Activity
Where's your evidence

- In your notebook, write down three recent situations when you have felt especially stressed. Attempt to recall your thinking at those times. Then draw a line down the page and write 'Where's the evidence?' at the top of the right-hand column.

- You will ideally be looking for evidence to dispute your negativity. However, don't worry if sometimes you have evidence to support your worries. Coping skills kick in then – and you have already looked at these.

TRACK DOWN YOUR PERSONAL STRESS SOURCE

Be your own best friend

We don't always have a friend or colleague around to point our thinking into a more positive direction, so a good question to ask yourself in these circumstances is: 'If this was

> **Today you will learn ...**
>
> to be a buddy to yourself.

happening to my best friend, rather than to me, what would I say to them? What evidence would I point out to them to help them see that their thoughts or assessment of a situation were not 100% true?'

The answer you will probably come up with will usually be quite different to your own, negative self-talk. We are always so much wiser and more constructive about finding solutions for others than we are for ourselves!

So become your own best friend. Use the questions above regularly, and you will find that it will really help you resolve stressful problems.

If a friend made a statement you felt was possibly skewed – or just plain wrong! – you would look at the evidence with them as a natural process. So do this for yourself as well.

A question of balance

Unfortunately, when we are suffering from stress and the associated emotions of anxiety or depression, we tend to look for evidence to back up our negative thinking and discount the positive.

If we say 'Hello' to a colleague in the corridor at work and they walk past us without responding, in a poor frame of mind we see that as evidence that we are un-likeable or of no consequence. In a good frame of mind we would probably assume that our colleague was simply pre-occupied.

TRACK DOWN YOUR PERSONAL STRESS SOURCE

So check for evidence to support or dispute your negative thinking. This will help you begin to believe your more positive beliefs more strongly.

TOP TIP

- Advise yourself exactly as though you are advising your best friend.
- Get a balance between noticing both positive and negative events in the day, rather than focusing on the bad things.

Activity

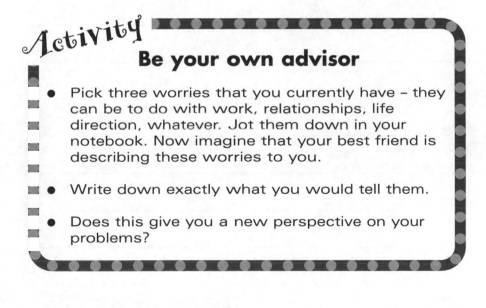

Be your own advisor

- Pick three worries that you currently have – they can be to do with work, relationships, life direction, whatever. Jot them down in your notebook. Now imagine that your best friend is describing these worries to you.

- Write down exactly what you would tell them.

- Does this give you a new perspective on your problems?

TRACK DOWN YOUR PERSONAL STRESS SOURCE

Your notes

....

....

....

....

....

....

....

....

....

....

....

....

....

....

CHAPTER 5

DE-STRESS USING
YOUR BODY

Calm down – but how?

> **Today you will learn ...**
>
> how body awareness can help you to beat stress.

One of the biggest worries for people who are aware that their lives are full of stress is the effect it may have on them physically. We have already discussed the fact that stress can be a contributory factor to certain illnesses. The other side of this coin is that our bodies will work very effectively with us to relieve stress.

Over the next few days, therefore, we will be looking at the wide variety of ways in which we can relieve stress through encouraging our body to help us out.

Recognising the signs

Remember the fight or flight mechanism that we discussed on Day 16? Our muscles contract and become tense under orders from the brain, which, in prehistoric times, was telling the body to prepare to fight a tiger (or run like hell away from one)! The tension was intended to be helpful to you – to keep you safer in dangerous situations.

The problem with messages between brain and body is that they tend to be very simple – just a sort of 'red alert' really. The body doesn't get told what the danger is, and therefore reacts in its pre-programmed way – ready to fight a tiger – even when the stressful event is nothing more than a disgruntled shop assistant being rude to you, or missing your train by a whisker.

DE-STRESS USING YOUR BODY

TOP TIP

- ◆ Muscular tension is the body's response to 'danger' signals from the brain.
- ◆ Our bodies still operate on the old 'sabre-tooth in the bushes' premise.
- ◆ Don't be alarmed by the initial physical symptoms that arise with stress and anxiety. They are not harmful (unless perhaps you have a cardiac condition).

Activity

Recognise your physical symptoms

● Think about times that you feel especially stressed. What physical symptoms do you notice? These vary for each of us, but jot down those that you encounter regularly – this might include:

- – tightness in your stomach,
- – your heart racing,
- – shortness of breath,
- – sweating,
- – dizziness,
- – clammy hands.

DE-STRESS USING YOUR BODY

Learn to be aware of tension

Learning to recognise the bodily tension we looked at yesterday is the first step to releasing it.

Today's activity will help you do that.

> **Today you will learn ...**
>
> how to become more specifically aware of tension in your body.

Using your notebook, copy out an empty version of the schedule below, and fill it in on a daily basis for a week. We'll call this your 'tension awareness record.' Some examples are given to start you off.

TENSION AWARENESS RECORD		
Date		
Time	**Stressor**	**Physical reaction**
7.30 am	Train is cancelled.	Tenseness in neck and shoulders.
11.15 am	Manager asks to see me regarding work I know I have done badly.	Tightness in stomach.
2.45 pm	Huge amount of paperwork to deal with by 5 pm.	Slight headache.
4.45 pm	Can see will not get away in time for reasonable train.	Headache worsens.
6.00 pm	Race to station. Train packed to rafters. No seats. Smoky. Am not going to get home in time to get to Parents' Evening.	Pounding headache, tightness in stomach.

DE-STRESS USING YOUR BODY

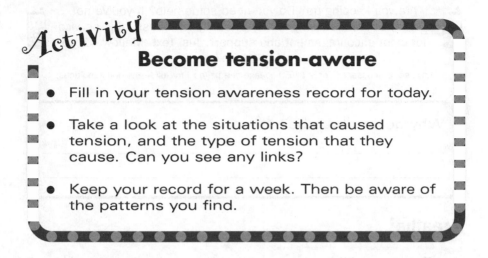

Activity

Become tension-aware

- Fill in your tension awareness record for today.

- Take a look at the situations that caused tension, and the type of tension that they cause. Can you see any links?

- Keep your record for a week. Then be aware of the patterns you find.

Different events cause different tensions

You will notice that certain events – for example, personal confrontations – trigger tension in your stomach. Events that trigger irritability – for example, a heavy workload – tend to produce tension in the head, leading to headaches.

The first step is to become used to being aware of the types of tension you feel, and when and why you feel them. You then have the opportunity of using one of the many skills you are learning to reduce the stress to manageable proportions, or to eliminate it altogether.

 TOP TIP

- You can increase your awareness of your body's responses, and notice how particular stresses result in predictable symptoms. Increased awareness will enable you to find ways to let go of the tension you discover.

DE-STRESS USING YOUR BODY

89

Are you keeping up? Do you need some help? If you've not already subscribed, why not try the daily text messaging service for extra encouragement and support. Just text 'Mellow 41' to 80881 now.

Each set of messages costs £1.50. Please see page xii for full terms and conditions.

Why do you breathe?

_____

_____

Breathe!

Today you will learn ...

that breathing is even more important than you thought!

You have probably written 'To stay alive' (or words to that effect).

Whilst staying alive is pretty important, and breathing is integral to achieving this, if that's all you think it achieves, you are missing out on all the other things that breathing can do for you!

What other things? Place a sheet of paper over the opposite page and jot down below any other ideas that you have.

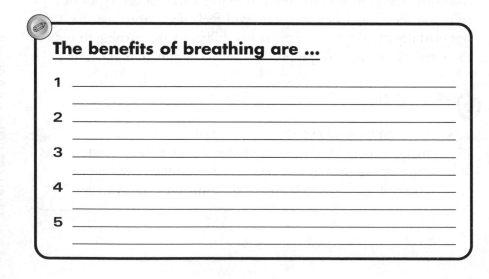

The benefits of breathing are ...

1 _____

_____

2 _____

_____

3 _____

_____

4 _____

_____

5 _____

_____

DE-STRESS USING YOUR BODY

If you thought of even three benefits, then you have done very well. Now take a look at all the many positives in favour of breathing well.

◆ It carries oxygen into our bloodstream. The bloodstream, in turn, then acts pretty much like a grocery delivery van, moving around the various parts of the body and providing them with the amounts of the stuff that they need to keep healthy.

◆ It carries oxygen to our brains. Want to think faster, better, at a higher level? Breathe better!

◆ It keeps our heart rate and blood pressure down.

◆ If you have studied yoga, you will have heard of the 'calming breath' – the idea that breathing is good for your soul as well as your body.

◆ And most importantly – for the purposes of managing stress – breathing helps you to relax.

TOP TIP

◆ It takes four minutes of deep breathing to replace the stale air in your lungs with fresh air.

Activity
Be aware of your breathing

● Whatever time of the day or evening you are reading this, simply begin to have more awareness of your breathing.

● Do you find that this awareness slows your breathing down at all?

DE-STRESS USING YOUR BODY

Breathing skills

Like many things in life, there is a good way to breathe and a bad way to breathe. Many of us do it the bad way!

This is because breathing is second nature: it just 'happens', and we don't waste too much time thinking about it or taking notice of the way we do it.

> **Today you will learn ...**
>
> that only 'good' breathing will de-stress you – and you probably aren't breathing well enough yet.

So the first thing to do is to start noticing how you breathe.

Checking it out

When you have a quiet moment give this a go.

- Find a bit of space somewhere and lie on the floor on your back, with your knees slightly bent, in a relaxing position.
- Place your right hand on your stomach, just where your waistline is.
- Place your left hand in the centre of your chest.
- Now, without changing your natural rhythm, simply breathe in and out, and look out for the hand that rises highest when you breathe in – is it your right hand (on your stomach) or your left hand (on your chest)?

This will tell you, in simple terms, whether you are a deep breather (when the hand on your stomach will lift the highest) or a shallow breather (when the hand on your chest will rise higher). Most people don't usually think about their breathing, and are shallow breathers.

Error messages that trick our bodies

Returning to the fight or flight analogy again, if we are going to run like the wind or fight to the death, our muscles need a lot of oxygen. So when our bodies get the 'red alert' signal from our brains their immediate goal is to get as much oxygen as possible. They achieve this by getting the oxygenated blood round our bodies at a really fast pace – and to do this, our bodies ask our hearts to 'increase that pump rate'. How do we speed up the heart rate? We speed up our breathing. And how do we breathe more quickly? We breathe more shallowly. Stress, anxiety, panic attacks, headaches, muscle tension and fatigue are all exacerbated by quick, shallow breathing.

Instead of taking deep, full breaths that come up from our diaphragm, we breathe in and out very quickly, using just the upper part of our chest.

TOP TIP

♦ Good breathing relaxes us, bad breathing stresses us.

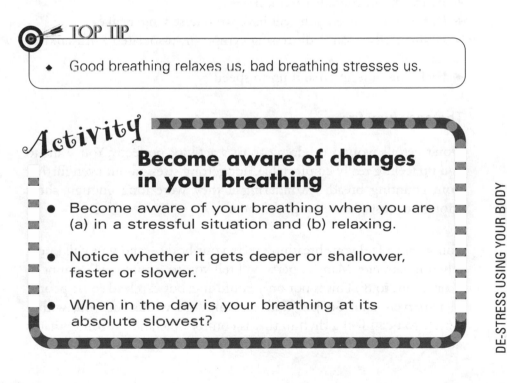

Activity

Become aware of changes in your breathing

● Become aware of your breathing when you are (a) in a stressful situation and (b) relaxing.

● Notice whether it gets deeper or shallower, faster or slower.

● When in the day is your breathing at its absolute slowest?

DE-STRESS USING YOUR BODY

More breathing skills

Of the many skills we teach our clients to reduce the physical symptoms of stress and anxiety, quite a number of them tell us that learning to control their breathing has been the most powerful of all.

> **Today you will learn ...**
>
> how to breathe brilliantly to reduce tension.

If you really could do only one simple thing to make a difference, we would recommend that this be it.

You can learn to breathe so brilliantly that you will be able, at will, to:

◆ Easily release muscular tension
◆ Become so relaxed you will have trouble staying awake
◆ Dramatically reduce distressing symptoms associated with anxiety states
◆ Feel more energised and up to speed.

The easy way first

Don't get all wound up doing today's activity perfectly. You want to end up feeling really comfortable, not getting stressed out even further from counting breaths, wondering if they were long enough, short enough or just plain enough of them.

You want to feel your breathing relax your body – and you will know when it happens. Many experts will tell you to 'count to 4', 'count to 6' or 'count to 8'. This is not only confusing, but can lead some people to hyperventilate! So just find a count that works for you, within which you can feel a rhythm that is comfortable and breathing that is slow and deep. Whatever works for you is fine.

Horizontal or vertical?

Another option, which you should decide for yourself, is whether you sit down or lie down. The advantage of practising deep breathing in a sitting position is that it can be done whenever and wherever you like – in the garden, on the train, even in a meeting if necessary.

When you are comfortable, you can begin.

1 Place your hands in the same positions as before (see Day 42).
2 Now breathe in slowly (count if you want to) through your nose.
3 Ensure as you do this that the hand on your stomach rises, and the hand on your chest remains as unmoving as possible.
4 Now exhale slowly (count again if this helps you) and as you do, feel the hand on your stomach gently fall back.

⊚← TOP TIP

♦ Breathing well is perhaps one of the most important skills you can use to reduce the physical symptoms of stress.

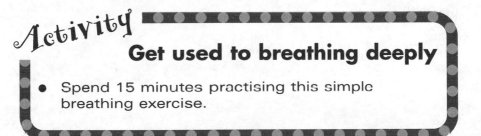

Activity

Get used to breathing deeply

● Spend 15 minutes practising this simple breathing exercise.

DE-STRESS USING YOUR BODY

Practising breathing

One of the weaknesses of skills such as good breathing is that people feel they can simply use them in a crisis.

Today you will learn ...

not to wait for a crisis to use this skill.

But if you wait for a crisis, you are not going to be skilled enough, or practised enough, to be able to use this tool on an almost unconscious, second-nature basis. You're going to have to run through the steps of yesterday's activity in your mind, try to remember what and in which order you do them all and, whoops! – too late, you're all wound up and in the manager's office.

 TOP TIP

A HIGHLY IMPORTANT POINT
◆ For instant stress reduction you need to practise breathing exercises on a **daily** basis.

Think about professional sportspeople. Their responses under pressure are so well rehearsed that they have become automatic. They don't have (or have the time) to think about kicking the ball before they are tackled, etc. – it has become a reflex response.

Good breathing to reduce stress in a difficult situation is the same. So practise!

A good rule

A good rule is the 'rule of 4' which is very easy to remember:

- Breathe in and out to a count of four.
- Do this for four minutes.
- Do it four times a day.

This is why:

1 Four is a 'middle of the road' number for counting breaths in and out – so it is handy to use.
2 Practising four times a day is also obvious – the more you do it, the easier it will become.
3 Doing it for four minutes actually has a lot going for it – it is not just a number picked out of thin air. In fact, it takes about four minutes for your lungs to do the job of getting the new oxygen into the capillaries that feed your circulatory system, and to remove the stale carbon dioxide.

TOP TIP

- Don't wait for a crisis – good breathing skills need to be second nature. Practise regularly.

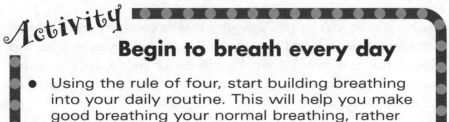

Activity

Begin to breath every day

- Using the rule of four, start building breathing into your daily routine. This will help you make good breathing your normal breathing, rather than simply 'crisis breathing'.

DE-STRESS USING YOUR BODY

'Know thyself.' Socrates

Your breathing schedule

If good, deep, relaxed breathing is
not reducing your stress and anxiety levels at all, then perhaps:

1 You have not done it often enough.
2 You have not done it for long enough.

Have you spent as much time practising as you think you have? You
can find out more about advanced breathing techniques either via the
internet, specialised books, or by taking yoga or meditation classes. You
will find these skills extremely helpful in your quest to reduce the
physical symptoms of stress.

TOP TIP

♦ Good breathing will relax you, ease muscular tension, and
diminish other physical symptoms of stress. It is not
difficult to master, but it does require regular practise.

Yoga

The benefits of yoga are probably already well known to you. Through
movement, breathing and body control, yoga helps you to relax and
relieve stress. It is said that just 15 minutes of yoga a day can enable
you to feel more relaxed, concentrate better and sleep more soundly.
Definitely worth a try!

Activity

Make breathing part of your schedule

- Make sure that by the end of today, you have practised your breathing skills at least twice. Remember to use the rule of four.

- For the first week, add your breathing exercises to your diary. You should also use your notebook to record the actual time at which you practised on a daily basis.

- After that, use the rule of four on a regular basis.

DE-STRESS USING YOUR BODY

Relaxing to reduce stress

Probably the most common phrase we hear from friends and colleagues when we begin to look frazzled round the edges and steam comes out of our ears is, 'Just relax!'

> **Today you will learn ...**
>
> about a very simple form of relaxation.

In the midst of a frantic day at work, or stuck in a ten-mile tailback when you should have been somewhere important half an hour ago – how **do** you relax?

When we teach breathing skills to relieve the physical symptoms of stress, we always teach relaxation skills as well. Together, these two techniques form an extremely effective barrier to stress, or – if stress has already crept up on you – using these two skills will reduce it speedily and dramatically.

Your number one simplest relaxation technique

Yawning! Whilst we tend to think yawning simply indicates tiredness or boredom, on many occasions it is actually helping to relieve stress. It ensures more oxygen enters our lungs and moves into our bloodstream, de-tensing muscles and de-stressing our brains.

So if you feel a yawn coming on, and you have enough privacy, don't stifle it – use it as the ultra-deep breath that it is and let it flow right through you.

TOP TIP

◆ Yawning is not advisable at dinner parties or Promotion Board meetings.

DE-STRESS USING YOUR BODY

Other techniques

Unless you live on a deserted island, you may have spent many hours reading magazine and newspaper articles, as well as books and internet articles, on how to relax. You may be confused by the number of different approaches to relaxation. These can include:

◆ Lying on a mat thinking about faraway places
◆ Playing an audio tape of someone speaking to you in a soothing voice
◆ Making your own tape
◆ Listening to the sounds of waves, or jungle noises.

If any of these work for you, that's wonderful and we encourage you to continue with whatever helps you relax. However, a weakness of these methods can be that you cannot use them **at will**. Tomorrow you will learn some more relaxation techniques.

TOP TIP

◆ Relaxation and breathing together will dramatically reduce the physical symptoms of stress.
◆ Use a yawn as a simple relaxer.

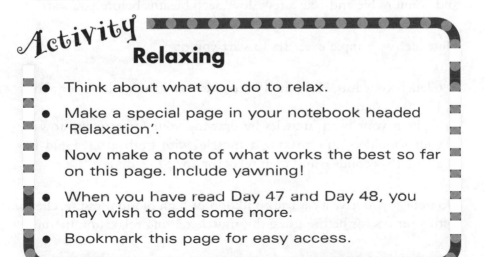

Activity **Relaxing**

● Think about what you do to relax.

● Make a special page in your notebook headed 'Relaxation'.

● Now make a note of what works the best so far on this page. Include yawning!

● When you have read Day 47 and Day 48, you may wish to add some more.

● Bookmark this page for easy access.

DE-STRESS USING YOUR BODY

Relaxation exercises

Whilst some of the relaxation solutions listed yesterday may work well for you, our experience with clients has shown us that muscle relaxation techniques give more immediate and visible benefits.

Today you will learn ...

some skills to help you relax at will.

These techniques also have the huge advantage of relaxing you very quickly and can be used in almost any situation.

Progressive muscle relaxation involves tensing and relaxing, in succession, fifteen different muscle groups of the body.

The idea is to tense each muscle group hard for about 10 seconds, and then let go of it suddenly, enjoying the sensation of limpness. Allow the relaxation to develop for at least 15–20 seconds before going on to the next group of muscles. Notice how the muscle group feels when relaxed, in contrast to how it felt when tensed. You might also say to yourself, 'relax', as you do so. Make sure you are in a setting that is quiet and comfortable and take a few slow, deep breaths before you start.

Here are two simple exercises to start you off.

- ◆ Clench your fists. Hold for 10 seconds – and then release for about 15–20 seconds.
- ◆ Tighten your bicep muscles by drawing your forearms up toward your shoulders and 'making a muscle' with both arms. Hold for about 10 seconds – and then relax for 15–20 seconds.

Do note, if you have a cardiac condition or high blood pressure, check with your doctor before using this muscle tensing relaxation method.

DE-STRESS USING YOUR BODY

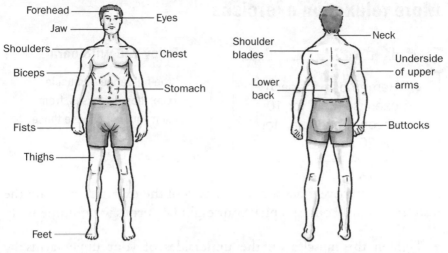

Forehead
Eyes
Jaw
Shoulders
Chest
Biceps
Stomach
Fists
Thighs
Feet

Neck
Shoulder blades
Underside of upper arms
Lower back
Buttocks

Fifteen different muscle groups of the body.

TOP TIP

♦ Tensing and then relaxing your muscles is a very powerful form of relaxation.

Activity

Time for your exercises

● Practise these two exercises. Do each of them several times to give yourself the idea of tensing and relaxing. Feel the relaxation flow through your body.

● You may find this hard at first, but keep practising until it becomes easier.

DE-STRESS USING YOUR BODY

More relaxation exercises

Today you will learn ...

the full range of muscle relaxation exercises, from which you can choose those best for you.

Now that you have practised one or two of the exercises, here are the rest. Try them all out, and pick your eight favourites to continue with.

♦ Tighten the muscles on the undersides of your upper arms by extending your arms out straight and locking your elbows. Hold – then relax.

♦ Tighten your forehead muscles by raising your eyebrows as high as you can. Hold – then relax.

♦ Open your mouth so widely that you stretch the muscles around the hinges of your jaw. Hold – then relax. Let your lips part and let your jaw hang loose.

♦ Screw up the muscles around your eyes, clenching them tightly shut. Hold – then relax.

♦ Tighten the muscles in the back of your neck by gently pulling your head way back, as if you were going to touch your head to your back. Focus only on tensing your neck muscles. Hold – then relax.

♦ Tighten your shoulders by raising them up as if you were going to touch your ears. Hold – then relax.

♦ Tighten the muscles around your shoulder blades by pushing your shoulder blades back as if you were going to touch them together. Hold – then relax.

♦ Tighten the muscles of your chest by taking in a deep breath. Hold – then relax.

♦ Tighten your stomach muscles by sucking your stomach in. Hold – then relax. Imagine a wave of relaxation spreading through your abdomen.

- Tighten your lower back by arching it up. (Omit this exercise if you have lower back pain.) Hold – then relax.
- Tighten your buttocks by pulling them together. Hold – then relax. Imagine the muscles in your hips going loose and limp.
- Squeeze the muscles of your thighs all the way down to your knees. Hold – then relax. Feel your thigh muscles smoothing out and relaxing completely.
- Tighten your feet by curling your toes downward. Hold – then relax.

Finally, imagine a wave of relaxation slowly spreading throughout your body, starting at your head and gradually penetrating every muscle group all the way down to your toes.

Do your favourite eight muscle groups every day for a week. At the end of the week, pick the best four. For the next week, do these four every day. Then pick your best two. Do these two every day for a week. Now you have the option of keeping two up your sleeve, or reducing to one firm favourite.

This 'favourite' will be the relaxation exercise that allows you to relax at will and quite instantaneously. Any time. Any place.

Along with deep breathing, you now have two tools that you can use easily and anywhere to bring down your stress levels physically.

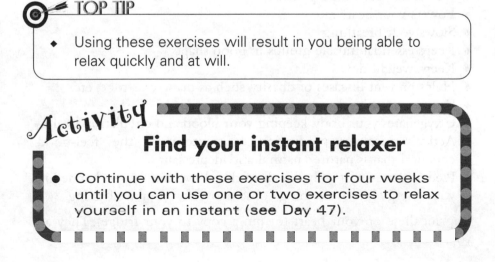

◎ TOP TIP

- Using these exercises will result in you being able to relax quickly and at will.

Activity
Find your instant relaxer

- Continue with these exercises for four weeks until you can use one or two exercises to relax yourself in an instant (see Day 47).

DE-STRESS USING YOUR BODY

Getting physical

Here are two questions: how many good reasons for taking exercise can you list and how much exercise, per week, do you take? Cover the rest of this page first, and then write your own answers below.

> **Today you will learn ...**
>
> whether you are an exerciser or a couch potato – and why the difference is important.

Exercise is good for me because ...	Exercise I take per week (type, time spent) ...
_____	_____
_____	_____
_____	_____
_____	_____
_____	_____

Feeling good

You may have listed things such as 'staying healthy' and 'feel-good factor' in the first column. You are quite right, of course, but you will be more motivated to exercise, and appreciate its positive impact better, if you are more specifically aware of its benefits. Exercise:

◆ Decreases your blood pressure
◆ Lowers your heart rate
◆ Slows your breathing
◆ Keeps essential muscle groups in good shape
◆ Keeps weight down
◆ Helps prevent diseases of obesity, such as diabetes, stroke, etc.
◆ Keeps energy levels up
◆ Oxygenates your body, keeping your blood and circulation healthy
◆ Actively increases production of serotonin – the 'feel-good' chemical that is nature's natural anti-depressant
◆ Reduces stress not only via all of the above, but by re-channelling your energy into something constructive for your well-being.

Imprint these on your heart (or pin a copy to your fridge). They are your motivators.

DE-STRESS USING YOUR BODY

So what do you do?

Only you can decide on the best form of exercise for yourself (What sports do you like? Is there a gym nearby?), but we urge you to build two things into whatever you choose.

1 **Timing** Ideally, 30 minutes × 3 times a week where your heart rate rises above its normal level.
2 **Consistency** Make sure that whatever you do, it is sustainable – you need to be thinking of exercise for life.

Some easy options

1 Stairs are your friends! Never take a lift unless absolutely necessary.
2 If you drive to work, can you park a little further away from your office? If so, do, and walk the rest of the way.
3 If your workplace happens to be within walking distance – up to half an hour away on foot – then once or twice a week, leave the car at home.
4 Get a bike. Use it whenever you can.
5 Sack the gardener.
6 Pick a half-hour TV programme you really enjoy, and plan a small exercise routine that you can do while watching it.

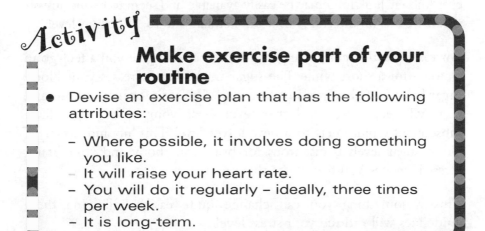

Activity

Make exercise part of your routine

- Devise an exercise plan that has the following attributes:

  – Where possible, it involves doing something you like.
  – It will raise your heart rate.
  – You will do it regularly – ideally, three times per week.
  – It is long-term.

DE-STRESS USING YOUR BODY

You are what you eat

When you are feeling really stressed, rushed, late, out of conrol – what do you choose to eat?

Today you will learn ...

if the food in your store cupboard is adding to your stress – and how to change this.

◆ Nothing.
◆ A chocolate bar.
◆ Whatever is in your desk drawer at the time, even if it is just a two-day old sandwich.
◆ A take-away sent in from the curry house / fish and chip shop / pizza outlet next door.

If you consider yourself to be a smart, healthy eater, feel free to move on to tomorrow's lesson. However, if you feel too stressed to worry about what you are eating, and if you choose any of the items above, then you need to know – what you eat is actually contributing to the stress in your life, not relieving it.

The food/mood relationship

In recent years, much more attention has been paid to the relationship between food and mood. We are currently eating the most stressful diet ever known. Junk food may be easily available, and seem to be the answer when we are 'on the run', but it can actually add to your stress levels.

For example, that comforting chocolate bar will give you a feel-good factor – for a short while. The sugar in the bar increases your blood sugar levels and gives you instant energy. But wait for half an hour and you will feel more tired than ever – as your blood sugar level subsequently plummets to a new, lower level. This 'up and down' of blood sugar levels is disastrous for both your body and your brain. Stress increases. You feel worse than ever.

This is something you can change quite easily. Following these guidelines will **reduce** your stress levels.

◆ Reduce (or eliminate altogether) all **sweet, sugary foods**. It really is not too strong a statement to say that sugar is, under normal circumstances, a poison! It does you no earthly good at all, and your energy levels will be much better sustained by the alternatives below.

◆ **Complex carbohydrates** can enhance your performance under stress by releasing energy consistently and slowly. You will find them in, for example, bran and oat-based cereals, wholemeal bread and pasta and brown rice.

◆ Eat one or two good helpings of **protein** daily. Get it from fish, chicken or lean meat. If you are a vegetarian or vegan, soya and tofu are good alternatives. These foods will really improve your mental functioning, and supply essential cell-repairing amino acids.

◆ You would have to live on another planet not to be aware of the 'Eat more **fruit and vegetables**' campaign. Ideally eaten raw, steamed or lightly cooked, and the darker the colour the better, fruit and veg provide your body with a host of stress-busting vitamins and nutrients.

◆ Eat **dairy products** in moderation. Whilst high in fat, they also provide protein, calcium and potassium, which are all excellent stress reducers and muscle relaxers. Stick to 'low fat' products where you can.

TOP TIP

- ◆ Attempt to eat well and regularly.
- ◆ Ensure that you have healthy snacks to hand so that you don't sabotage your efforts.

Activity
Clean up your diet

- Using your notebook, make a list of healthy snacks that appeal to you. Then hit the supermarket and ensure that you have good stocks of these items.

- Look back over the last week at what you ate. Write down what you now recognise as 'bad stuff'. Write down any 'good stuff' (from the above lists). What positive changes can you make?

DE-STRESS USING YOUR BODY

Are you keeping up? Do you need some help? If you've not already subscribed, why not try the daily text messaging service for extra encouragement and support. Just text 'Mellow 51' to 80881 now.

Each set of messages costs £1.50. Please see page xii for full terms and conditions.

The land of nod

Poor sleep patterns can be a symptom of stress. They can also be a cause of stress.

> **Today you will learn ...**
>
> how sleep problems – too little, too much, too restless – can affect you and how to improve your sleep pattern.

Tick any of the following statements that apply to you.

- I wake up in the morning feeling as tired as when I went to bed. ☐
- I never wake ahead of my alarm clock. ☐
- I always wake an hour or more ahead of my alarm clock and cannot return to sleep. ☐
- It takes me ages to get to sleep at night. ☐
- I wake several times in the night. ☐
- I rarely sleep more than 2 or 3 hours at a stretch. ☐
- I usually feel really tired by mid afternoon. ☐
- I often wake up at 3 am or 4 am and can't get back to sleep easily. ☐

If you ticked two or more statements, or if any one is a regular occurrence, then you need to develop a sleep routine to reduce the stress that is being created by lack of it.

Reset your body clock

Your body clock is a very simple mechanism. Without routine it simply goes haywire. Tempting though it might be to lie in, if you have lain awake for much of the night, tossing, turning and worrying, you still need to get up at exactly the same time every day. Your body needs regularity and consistency to correct itself. So if you feel sleep deprived, don't stay in bed longer to recuperate – even at weekends. Your body will learn to take the extra sleep it needs at the end of the day, rather than at the beginning, and you will become less of a 'toss and turn' victim.

DE-STRESS USING YOUR BODY

Bed = sleep

Your mind needs to learn that bedtime does not equal reading, watching TV, doing the crossword, texting friends. Bedtime = sleep time. If you want to do any of the above, do them before you go to bed, not in or from your bed.

Get comfy

How comfortable is your bed? You won't enjoy a good night's sleep on a lumpy mattress, or one that's too hard or too soft.

Am I getting enough sleep?

Don't lie awake worrying about this! Anything between 6–9 hours falls within the 'normal' range. More or less than this occasionally is also OK.

How warm do I need to be?

For the best sleep, you want to have warm covers, but a cool room. Unless you fear burglars, some ventilation is good.

Make your bedroom inviting

There is no joy in climbing into bed over heaps of clothes, clutter and hobby-related items. If you can create a tranquil environment, your mind will absorb this and bedtime will become something you actually look forward to.

TOP TIP

- Oversleeping is as bad for you, if not worse, than not getting enough sleep. It will make you lethargic.
- Poor sleep can be both a symptom of and a cause of stress.
- Check you aren't consuming too much caffeine in coffee or tea.

Activity Banish bad sleep

- Using your notebook, start keeping a sleep record. You will need to do this for at least two weeks, possibly longer. Note patterns in wakefulness and what may have caused them – late nights out, lack of routine, alcohol, uncomfortable, too hot/cold etc. You can then use this sleep diary to make appropriate adjustments.

DE-STRESS USING YOUR BODY

Your notes

CHAPTER 6

DE-STRESS THROUGH ORGANISATION

Are you (dis)organised?

Do you feel that you are permanently in a state of chaos? Do you look around you at piles of paperwork, turn up on the wrong day for appointments, have no clue as to where you would find your bank statements or utility bills?

> **Today you will learn ...**
>
> how organised you are.

Are you one of the many people who purchase extended warranties for electrical goods, only to have no idea at all where the warranty is when the appliance breaks down and you need it?

If so, you are not alone. Frustrating though it is, not being a Totally Organised Person is quite OK. (In fact, TOPs can be rather smug and infuriating.) However, there is a middle way, and you will need to find it if feeling and being disorganised is causing you great stress.

Why do think you are disorganised? Take a look at the following suggestions:

◆ I just don't know what to do to become an organised person.
◆ I do know, but it is all such an effort.
◆ If I had more time, I would be really well organised.
◆ Space would make the difference. There's nowhere to put stuff.
◆ It is impossible to get organised with my lifestyle – it's too complex and erratic.

How many apply to you? If none, you can move on to Day 61. However, the likelihood is, if you feel stressed, you will feel disorganised.

Clutter

Just consider clutter. Is it everywhere? Does it overwhelm you?

Lack of time

Do you really feel that you are doing too much, or are you not organising your time well enough?

DE-STRESS THROUGH ORGANISATION

Goal setting

Do you stumble along in a crisis-driven way, reacting rather than being pro-active? Does this hinder your progress?

Now ask yourself one very important question: 'At what point does disorganisation really hinder me?'

This is a very important question, and the answer will be different for all of us. There are top business people who run successful organisations with offices that look like rubbish tips. There are people who live in spotless houses whose lives are still very stressful – being perfect all the time can be very time-consuming.

You will have your own optimum organisational threshold, and you alone will know what that is. So you should apply the suggestions of the next few days on an 'as it suits you' basis. One size does not fit all.

TOP TIP

♦ Lack of organisation is a great contributor to stress. However, finding your own threshold is important, or achieving something you don't really care about could stress you out even more.

Activity

Are you disorganised?

● Simply ask yourself these questions. Write down the answer(s) to question number 2 in your notebook.

1. Do I consider myself to be disorganised?

2. In what way(s)?

DE-STRESS THROUGH ORGANISATION

Get yourself motivated

If you are going to make any organisational changes, you have got to:

◆ Really **want** to do it, or
◆ Have a big enough incentive to **make** you do it.

Reasons to get organised

Think about a less stressful life. You are learning that there are many, many ways of reducing stress, but failing to address being more organised will leave a big hole. What would the value be to you of being more organised? Write your answers below. Then give each item an effort rating of 1 to 10, with 10 being totally worth it, 1 being marginally worth it. (Examples might be, I will increase my productivity, I'll stop getting so frustrated, It will help me calm down.)

The value to me of being more organised would be ...

1 _____
   Effort rating _____
2 _____
   Effort rating _____
3 _____
   Effort rating _____

If your effort ratings are over 7, you will have good motivation to change. If they are under 7, you may need some incentives.

Reward yourself

You could reward yourself for getting a job done by a certain date. Perhaps a pair of theatre tickets for a show you want to see, or a sporting event you are keen on. This technique works with children, and we really should use it a lot more as adults.

Or pay a price

However, sometimes a penalty can be a great incentive as well. Tell yourself you don't get to go out on Friday evening unless your desk at home (or work, or whatever) is tidy and up to date. Stick to it! This might be easier if you get your partner to be firm with you when you weaken.

Blab about it

The more people you tell of your plans, the more likely you are to follow through (shame is a great motivator!)

Use embarrassment

In fact, using shame can be a helpful tool for getting organised at home. Invite some guests over around the time you plan to finish clearing up your living area and you will have excellent motivation to stick with it.

Schedule it

We usually attend appointments that we have in our diaries. Use an 'appointment system' to build in time for getting organised. Schedule two hours, for example, on Saturday morning for clearing out the garage. This will work a great deal better than simply planning to find the time at some point.

TOP TIP

- Work out what motivates you best, and use this to get more organised in specific areas.
- Tell as many people as possible of your plans. Ask them to help you stick to them.

Activity
Motivate yourself

- Think of at least two things that will motivate you into action.
- Now use your notebook to decide what you would like to use these motivators to achieve in the next week.

DE-STRESS THROUGH ORGANISATION

Overcome procrastination

Most of us procrastinate some of the time, especially if:

◆ The job is unpleasant
◆ We don't believe we are up to it
◆ We are pessimistic about the outcome and how we will deal with it.

In such circumstances, we become experts in finding a host of tasks to do that 'must' be done first. On other occasions, we simply have so many tasks to deal with that we become frozen with indecision, and find it almost impossible to make a start on anything at all.

If any of the above rings bells with you, you are probably a good procrastinator, and – as a result – live with the chronic stress that failing to deal with things in good time brings with it.

Displacement activities (procrastination in disguise)

What happens when something you are finding really hard to tackle has a deadline beginning to tick away? Are any of the following activities those that you find a need to undertake?

◆ A major desk or drawer tidy-up
◆ A session deleting unwanted emails
◆ Sharpening your pencils
◆ Having a quick game of Solitaire on the computer
◆ Making endless cups of coffee
◆ Checking every few minutes or so for new e-mails/text messages
◆ Doodling
◆ Making a long 'to do' list and working on the most unimportant items on the list.

The illusion of usefulness

The only reason that procrastination seems to help is that it prevents us from focusing on the main task, thus temporarily reducing our stress levels. However, as the time ticks away, stress levels rise even higher when the task moves no further forward to completion.

Fight it

Your stress levels will rise and rise the more time you waste staring out of the window or unbending paperclips. So get active, and make yourself overcome procrastination. Here are some suggestions:

◆ Build in a reward. 'Once I have done this task I will treat myself to …'
◆ Break the task down into small steps. For example, if you have the whole house to clean, adopt a 'one room a day' approach. Don't think of the whole, but just what you can easily achieve.
◆ Stop worrying ahead of time. Save your energies for when you actually have to do the task. If you find yourself worrying in advance, silently shout 'Stop' in your head.
◆ Challenge negative thoughts (re-read Chapters 2 and 3 if you need to). Don't simply give yourself permission to have thoughts such as, 'I'll never get this right,' 'I cannot complete the task in the time.' Find positive alternatives to these thoughts.
◆ Prioritise and stick to your list. Don't allow yourself to get distracted until you have completed as much as you need to that is at the top of your list.

⊙⟜◄ TOP TIP

◆ We need to employ a variety of tactics to keep procrastination at bay, and to work hard at these.

𝒜ctivity ●●●●●●●●●●●●
Stop dithering

● Jot down what plan you could make or tactics you might use to prevent procrastination happening again in your life.

DE-STRESS THROUGH ORGANISATION

Organising your time

Are you one of those people who would like an eight-, or even ten-day week in which to get through everything? If so, you are not alone.

Why don't we manage our time better?

Actually, most of us don't manage our time at all – except in some vague sort of 'I'll try and find time for that on Sunday' way. We simply press on – until we feel swamped, and our stress rates rise through the roof.

How time stressed are you?

Rate each of the following statements 0 (= never), 1 (= not often), 2 (= some of the time) or 3 (= all of the time). Add up your score at the end.

I feel that: Rating

- I don't have enough time for leisure pursuits.   _____
- I don't give my family the time I would like.   _____
- I always feel behind with chores and tasks.   _____
- I cannot do my job well in the time that I have.   _____
- I cannot say 'no' when people make time demands on me.   _____
- I rarely ask others for help when over-worked.   _____
- I am often late for meetings and appointments.   _____
- I get irritated with people who simply want to chat.   _____
- I rarely see my friends.   _____
- No-one seems to understand how busy I am.   _____

0–10: In the normal range.
10–20: You need to tighten up your time management.
20–30: You need to completely re-vamp your time management.

DE-STRESS THROUGH ORGANISATION

Improve your time management

For one week, keep a time log. It will look something like this.

Date			
Time	Activity	Time taken	Value of use of time
7.20 am	Lay awake in bed.	20 mins	Could have got up sooner.
8.00 am	Rush to get ready for work.	30 mins	Would have had more time if had got up sooner.
8.45 am	Queue for cappuccino.	10 mins	Kick starts my day, so happy to give time to that.
9.15 am	Get rid of small tasks from list on desk.	45 mins	Waste of time – could have delegated and spent time on project.

If you keep a time log regularly for a week you will begin to see how you can re-organise your day, cut out waste and, who knows, may even find that you have time for a little fun!

From now on, work with a weekly planner alongside a priorities list and put the important tasks in first. Once you have allowed adequate time for them, you can slot in unimportant tasks and social activities – there will be time for these with good time management.

TOP TIP

- ◆ Managing time is vital when you feel stressed.
- ◆ It is your best resource, don't squander it.
- ◆ Stick as closely as you can to a written weekly plan for major tasks.

Activity **Start managing your time**

- ● Start your first daily time log.

DE-STRESS THROUGH ORGANISATION

Setting your goals

Considering how simple and effective goal-setting is, it is surprising that more of us don't use it as a regular tool.

> **Today you will learn ...**
>
> the importance and principles of goal-setting.

For most of us, even when we set goals, they often go awry.

If this happens to you, it could be because:

- Your goals were unrealistic.
- You set yourself too many.
- You found you didn't want your goals badly enough.

Goal-setting weaknesses

One weakness of goal-setting, is that we make our goals too vague. If I say, 'I want to lose weight', I will probably not achieve it.

Write it down

Research has shown that those who write their goals down on paper, are much more likely to achieve them.

Be specific

Goals only become meaningful when they are **specific**. In this instance, I would need to be able to tell you:

- How much weight I wanted to lose
- When I intended to lose it by (e.g. a friend's wedding date)
- What type of diet I planned to go on
- How I would manage eating out
- How often I would food shop.

Suddenly, the goal becomes real and achievable.

Break it down

We fail with many of our goals simply because they are too big, too far away, too hard to achieve. Set achievable goals.

Use a realistic time frame

If we asked you to run the marathon with us and said it was next Monday, you would most likely turn us down. If we said it was next year, you might consider it. Why? Because the time frame is realistic.

Action plan

Goal	Action
On-going (daily)	
Short-term (1wk–1 mth)	
Medium-term (1mth–1yr)	
Long-term (over 1yr)	

Use your action plan to work out your needs, and list the action you need to take in order to achieve them very specifically.

⊚ TOP TIP

- ◆ Goals need to be specific if you are to achieve them.

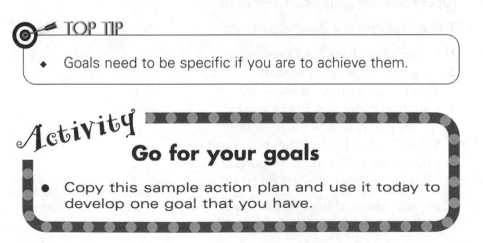

Activity
Go for your goals

- Copy this sample action plan and use it today to develop one goal that you have.

DE-STRESS THROUGH ORGANISATION

Clutter control

Clutter is an unusual stress trigger, in that it is not actually active. It is simply there. Many people manage to successfully:

Today you will learn ...

how to reduce your stress-inducing clutter.

◆ Ignore it
◆ Not mind it
◆ Actively like it all around them.

However, for most people, a cluttered environment seems to jam up their brains and cause all kinds of stress and anxiety. For these people clutter signifies:

◆ Inability to retain control
◆ A feeling of being overwhelmed
◆ Fear that something really important may be buried in the morass
◆ The old 'What is wrong with me?' question that looms whenever what seems like our complete inability to get our environment sorted out makes itself evident.

Most cluttered people do have a plan. You may have one yourself. You may have a list that has all your de-clutter projects written on it – 'Clean out garage,' 'Take bags of old clothes to charity,' 'Tidy all cupboards,' 'Get large pile of office filing up to date.'

Accept that you are fooling yourself. Writing things down on bits of paper is not the same as actually doing it!

Top excuses for not de-cluttering are:

1 It may come back into fashion.
2 I could need it again some day.
3 When I have time, I'll mend it.
4 One of the children might want it.
5 A messy desk makes me look busy.
6 When I retire I'll have time to read those.
7 I'm too busy with more important stuff.
8 I'll do a car boot sale/get on to ebay one day.

The point about clutter is that if you don't deal with it ruthlessly, it spreads. It is not static. It gets worse.

DE-STRESS THROUGH ORGANISATION

Techniques for decluttering

◆ Set a semi-regular de-clutter time. Decide on, say, 2 hours a week, and pick a day and time slot where you are usually free.

◆ Choose it or lose it. This can be a very hard choice. But to make it easier, set up a 'pending space.' This might be your garage, your garden shed, or your spare bedroom. Allow yourself a cooling-off period before taking things to the tip.

◆ Call a charity or the Scouts. Tell them that on such-and-such a date, you will have bag loads of second-hand items that they may be able to sell or use. This commitment will be a great motivator.

◆ Hire a skip. Another time-frame motivator. Set aside a weekend in the future, and book the skip to arrive the day before.

The hardest things to get rid of are often mementos. When just looking at old stuff brings back fond memories, it is hard to bin it. However, there are two possibilities here:

◆ Keep a sample. You don't need to keep every piece of hippy or punk clothing that you have collected – just one pair of flared pants or one black shirt will be just as evocative.

◆ Take a photo. For example – keeping the children's old bikes or other toys clogs up space; a photo doesn't.

TOP TIP

◆ Get started – Rome wasn't built in a day. Don't say that you won't start because you might not finish.

Make a start on clearing your clutter

● Using the above suggestions, and any more that you have of your own, write in your notebook a de-clutter action plan.

● Then pick one small item – a kitchen drawer for example – and tidy it up. How do you feel?

DE-STRESS THROUGH ORGANISATION

Prioritising and delegating

Prioritising

Like most people, you probably have a 'to do' list – but do you rate this list in order of priorities, as opposed to simply working through it? A lot of people don't.

Today you will learn ...

how prioritising and delegating will reduce stress.

This is partly because one way of feeling that we are keeping on top of tasks is by crossing as many of them off our 'to do' list as we can. In order to achieve this, we stick with completing the quick and easy tasks. This makes the list look good, but fails to get the longer, trickier, more important tasks done.

Start prioritising your 'to do' list as follows:

1 Important and urgent: high priority
2 Important but not urgent: medium priority
3 Urgent but not important: low priority
4 Neither urgent nor important: don't waste your time!

An important point to note is that, although 'Important but not urgent' has been given medium priority, one of the mistakes we make is not to spend enough time in this area. We are so busy fire-fighting in box 1 that we never have time to expand or enrich our lives or our businesses. What tasks do you think might come under the heading of 'Important but not urgent'? Jot down a few examples.

If you have got the right idea, you will have listed learning new skills, developing ideas, and so on. All things that may not have 'urgent' marked on them, but which you should find time for in order to expand the horizons of your life and enjoy it more.

Delegating

Most of us under pressure delegate far too little. Underneath this reluctance often lurks the old maxim, 'I can do it better/quicker myself.' Often, that is quite true – to begin with. But if you do the same task ten times, that's a lot of time. Take a couple of times to go slower as you show someone else how to do it, and you don't need to do it at all the other eight times.

Here's how to delegate:

◆ Do it genuinely. Don't hover in the background watching and worrying. That will be more stressful than ever (for both of you).
◆ Select someone you trust to get the job at least half right. You can teach them the rest.
◆ Even if the job isn't quite up to scratch, ask yourself, 'Does that really matter?' You are probably delegating less important tasks in any event.
◆ Be very appreciative. Praise what they have done well – you want them to help you more often, not less often in the future.
◆ If you really cannot get help from below, get it from above. Ask your line manager to recommend someone who might like to learn or have some spare time. He or she will be more aware of any 'slack' in the bigger picture.
◆ Use the same skills at home with your family. Children love to help and it is excellent for development of responsibility. If it's not as good as you would have done, so what. The rewards of delegating to children are huge.

TOP TIP

- Don't just have a 'to do' list – prioritise it.
- Learn to delegate – something done not quite as well as you would have done it is better than a nervous breakdown.

Activity
Reducing your 'to do' list

- Get out your 'to do' list and prioritise it.

- From the 'low priority' section of the list, pick at least one task and delegate it **now**.

- Begin to get used to doing this on a regular basis.

DE-STRESS THROUGH ORGANISATION

Organise your paperwork

'Clutter' – which we have discussed already – to many people means 'paperwork'. Even in these days of electronic communications and 'paper-free offices', for most of us, the barrage of paperwork that drops onto our doormat seems relentless and unstoppable.

Most of us flounder in a sea of paperwork because we do not act instantly. Advertisers are very cunning. They don't want you to bin their unsolicited mail – so they try every trick in the book to get you to look at it and hang on to it.

> **Today you will learn ...**
>
> surfacing when hidden beneath a mass of papers.

The old 'I might need to know about that / use that / buy one of those one day' thought is what keeps paper piling up around us.

Do you rip articles out of magazines with alluring titles such as, '50 ways to look thinner,' 'How to banish greenfly,' 'Sell your second-hand car for more than you paid for it' etc? You are not alone. But this isn't helpful.

◎◢ TOP TIP

> ◆ Once you start collecting paperwork, throwing it away is emotionally harrowing. So don't collect it in the first place.

Give this a go instead:

◆ Keep a small basket in a corner of your hallway and immediately put all junk mail in it.
◆ Open all other mail straight away and bin anything that does not need a response.

- Charity requests are hard just to ditch, so collect them in a box, and once every few weeks or months (depending on your bank balance) get one of your children to 'lucky dip' one out of the box, and send a small sum to that particular charity. Bin the rest and start again.
- Have an efficient filing system. A good idea is to do your filing only once every 3 months (say). Store it in a tray or box until then. When you come to do it, you will find that 50% of the paperwork you thought, 3 months ago, needed keeping, can actually be thrown away. Then file the important things that are left.
- Don't have too many files. Keeping a file labelled 'Hernia operation possibilities' is too specific (unless you are about to have a hernia operation). Just have one 'Health advice, general' file.
- Keep a small, fireproof, safety deposit box for vital papers like birth certificates, house deeds, your will, share certificates and passports. Then you will always know where the really important things are – as will your family, if necessary.
- Keep a large wicker basket next to your waste bin in your kitchen/utility area. Throw all papers and magazines into it as soon as they are read. This saves them from cluttering up coffee tables, but you still have access to them for a few days if you recall something urgent that you wanted to look at.

TOP TIP

- Paperwork can multiply quickly and become difficult to discard. Deal with it immediately.

Activity

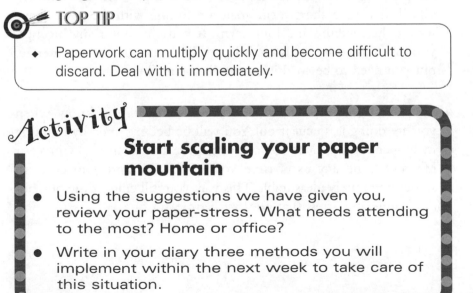

Start scaling your paper mountain

- Using the suggestions we have given you, review your paper-stress. What needs attending to the most? Home or office?

- Write in your diary three methods you will implement within the next week to take care of this situation.

DE-STRESS THROUGH ORGANISATION

Keeping up the good work

> **Today you will learn ...**
>
> how to stay organised and avoid
> slipping back into old ways.

Staying organised may be as difficult as getting organised. Don't run the risk of simply sinking back into disorganisation by becoming passive.

Use your notebook to make a list of all the methods that work for you, and that you intend to keep on doing. Think less in terms of how to organise your complex life so that it works a little better, and more in terms of how to simplify your life through organisation, so that you have more time, a tidier environment and clearer goals.

Here are some final tips and reminders to keep you on the straight and narrow:

◆ Keep your goals in the forefront of your mind – write them down. Check that your short-term goals are in line with those you have set for the medium and long term. If you encounter any hiccups, you can adjust your goals accordingly. They are not cast in concrete, but you need to be working towards them all the time.

◆ Keep track of time-wasting and procrastination. You know when you are doing it, so cut it out. You will be better served by building in longer time periods for achieving the important tasks in your life, and using any extra time you have to reward yourself with something purely pleasurable. This way, you still enjoy 'time out' but don't suffer the stress that goes with time-wasting.

DE-STRESS THROUGH ORGANISATION

◆ You must learn to say 'no' and to delegate. Don't turn into a frazzled wreck by a) not being firm and b) not accepting that others can do tasks, maybe not quite as well as you, but close enough.

◆ Ensure that you live and work in an environment that doesn't stress you out because it is messy, noisy or irritating to you in any other way. Work at keeping it the way you want it. Be ruthless with clutter.

◆ Do two tasks at once where you can. For example, you can toast your bread whilst talking on the phone, or pedal an exercise bike while watching TV.

◆ Invest in good storage.

TOP TIP

◆ Once organised, stay organised!

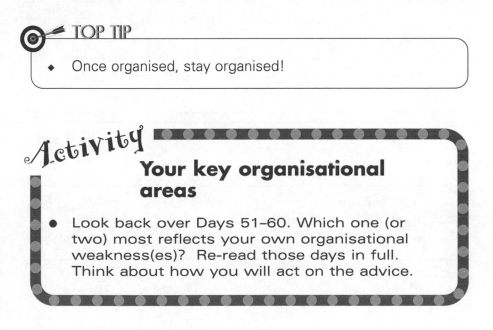

Activity

Your key organisational areas

● Look back over Days 51–60. Which one (or two) most reflects your own organisational weakness(es)? Re-read those days in full. Think about how you will act on the advice.

DE-STRESS THROUGH ORGANISATION

Your notes

CHAPTER 7

OVERCOMING STRESS-RELATED ANGER

Are you keeping up? Do you need some help? If you've not already subscribed, why not try the daily text messaging service for extra encouragement and support. Just text 'Mellow 61' to 80881 now.

Each set of messages costs £1.50. Please see page xii for full terms and conditions.

How stress causes anger

> **Today we will look at …**
>
> whether stress is raising your anger levels.

How much of your stress do you think is caused by the fact that you get angry quite quickly and easily? How much of your anger do you think is caused by stress?

Whichever way you look at it, if you find yourself getting angry, quite quickly, a lot of the time, you have a problem and need to deal with it. Not only is anger very stressful, it can ruin both personal and professional relationships, as well as being detrimental to your health.

Anger can also kill

Road rage is an example. An otherwise rational man or woman, when getting 'cut up' by another driver, becomes so angry that he/she decides to get his/her own back by giving chase. An accident results that kills two of the people involved.

21st century intolerance

We are more concerned than ever with our 'rights' (fuelled, very often, by our compensation culture). We are less philosophical, less inclined to put things down to experience. If our demands are not now met in a way that we have come to expect, we become angry.

Others get angrier as well

As we become generally angrier – so do others.

Suppressing anger

Expressing anger is becoming less acceptable, especially in the workplace. This means that by expressing anger inappropriately we may risk our jobs, or at least disciplinary action. We therefore often bottle anger up, instead of dealing with it, and this can be exceedingly harmful to both our emotional and physical well-being.

OVERCOMING STRESS-RELATED ANGER

Me? Angry?

One difficulty can be anger self-assessment. What may seem an angry response to person A is a natural way of dealing with situations to person B.

Are you aware of your own anger? Rate the following statements to check it out. Score your answers: 0 = never, 1 = occasionally, 2 = often.

Rating

- Others comment on my aggressive responses. _____
- Waiting in queues drives me mad. _____
- I can't tolerate rudeness. _____
- I always respond badly to criticism. _____
- I start arguments easily. _____
- Driving in traffic causes me huge stress. _____
- I consider most other drivers on the road to be bad drivers. _____
- I find most shop assistants, help lines, etc. quite incompetent. _____
- In difficult discussions with people, I tend to get most angry most quickly. _____
- I let petty annoyances really work me up. _____

0–7: Don't worry – you stay well-balanced in most tricky situations.

8–14: You are responding to stressful situations with anger too often.

15–20: Your angry responses may cause some serious damage if you don't make urgent changes.

TOP TIP

- Accepting that we do get inappropriately angry is half the battle to reducing such responses.

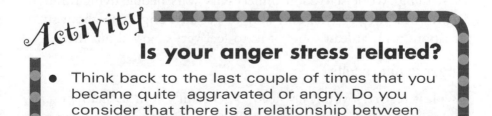

Activity
Is your anger stress related?

- Think back to the last couple of times that you became quite aggravated or angry. Do you consider that there is a relationship between your feeling angry and feeling stressed?

OVERCOMING STRESS-RELATED ANGER

When anger can be healthy

What would you say are the differences between healthy, constructive anger and unhealthy, destructive anger?

Have you ever thought of anger as being a good thing? Consider for a moment, and write down three or four suggestions below.

> **Today you will learn ...**
>
> that anger isn't always a bad thing – it is how you use it that matters.

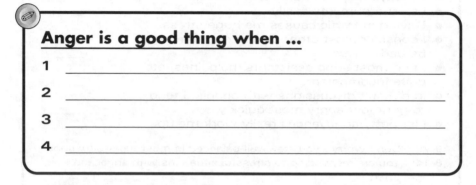

Anger is a good thing when ...

1 _____

2 _____

3 _____

4 _____

Let's take a look at some possibilities.

Anger at injustice

You see someone kicking a dog, hear on the news that innocent people in a far-off country are being brutally treated, notice someone at work who is always unfairly picked on by the boss ... These are situations where injustice prevails, and we need to get angry about these things. World starvation, unnecessary wars, people dying through lack of health care – the only way to get anything done about such situations is for at least some of us to feel very angry about them.

Anger to get results

As a **last resort**, if you really need to get results from recalcitrant staff, motor mechanics, waiters, your children, etc. then reasonable anger can work a treat.

Anger as a motivational tool

When you finally hear yourself say, 'Right. That's it. I'm not taking any more of this,' you know that you are going to blow your top in order to get some action. In a sense, you are bringing some energy to the situation.

Anger as a release

'Letting it all out' has actually been shown to have health benefits, compared to repressed anger, which we hold inside and which eats away at us. However, there are ways of letting things out which don't involve us becoming apoplectic, so use this with caution.

Anger as an alert signal

Healthy anger can be letting you know that something is wrong. You can use this alert to figure out what is worrying you, and then do something positive to change it. For example, if you find yourself becoming irritated every time you need to meet with a particular work colleague, ask yourself why they annoy you so. It may be that they are always late for your meetings, always dominate the discussion, regularly cancel at the last minute, etc. Becoming aware of your anger in these circumstances encourages you to change the situation so that it is less stressful.

TOP TIP

♦   Don't attempt to eliminate anger from your life. There are many ways in which healthy anger can be a helpful and motivating tool.

Activity

Is your anger helpful?

● Jot down two or three situations in which you became angry in the last week or two.

● Now think for a moment about the outcome. Do you feel that, in any of these instances, the anger achieved a good result? Does this help you to see when anger can actually be healthy?

OVERCOMING STRESS-RELATED ANGER

The anger spiral

Anger is built on our expectations regarding the ideals and behaviours of others. We expect people to treat us fairly and they don't. We expect them to be nice to us and they aren't. We expect them to help us and they walk away.

> **Today you will learn ...**
>
> how anger can escalate out of control.

Each time someone breaks a rule of ours, violates a contract or acts against our wishes, a possible option is to react with anger. But we don't have to – it is our choice.

Unfortunately, we do not always feel that we are in control of this choice – it is as though it has already been decided for us, and we act accordingly.

OVERCOMING STRESS-RELATED ANGER

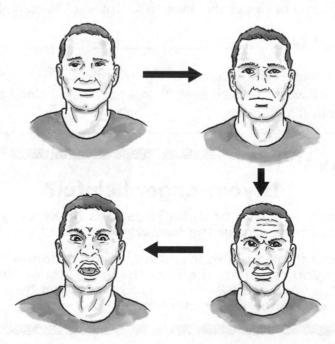

Earlier in this book, you did a lot of work on challenging your own thinking patterns. Now you can use these skills to help you to reduce your angry thoughts and feelings.

You understand well now the relationship between what we think and how we feel. A situation such as a rude boss may be the external trigger and our thought, 'My boss should not be rude to me' triggers the emotion of anger. It is the thought that drives the emotion – at least initially. However, once in the spiral, the emotion then drives further negative thoughts, such as, 'He really is a bully. He shouldn't be allowed to get away with it.' In turn, this makes you angrier than before – and so on, until the anger gets quite out of control. We make ourselves angry when our expectations of how others should behave are not met. This can lead us into an anger spiral which escalates the angry feelings that we have and makes situations worse.

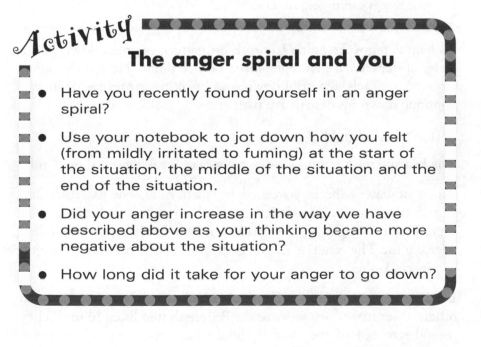

Activity
The anger spiral and you

- Have you recently found yourself in an anger spiral?

- Use your notebook to jot down how you felt (from mildly irritated to fuming) at the start of the situation, the middle of the situation and the end of the situation.

- Did your anger increase in the way we have described above as your thinking became more negative about the situation?

- How long did it take for your anger to go down?

OVERCOMING STRESS-RELATED ANGER

Getting out of the anger spiral

Let's take a look at someone who gets into an anger spiral – and learn from his mistakes! Over the next few days we'll use thought-challenging as our tool to see how we can help our guinea pig reduce his angry thoughts and responses.

> **Today you will learn ...**
>
> breaking the 'should' rule to reduce stress.

CASE STUDY

Peter is a 35-year-old computer specialist. He works in a high pressure job, feels stressed most of the time, and is perpetually offended by a myriad of slights and abuses. He is highly competitive and takes absolutely nothing lightly. In his mind, others are just out to annoy him, make his life difficult, and increase his stress – an indifferent shop assistant, a slow driver ahead of him, a leisurely bank clerk – any of these things can trigger his rage.

To help Peter, we're going to break his pattern of anger down into a series of steps. Each step represents a 'choice point'. He can choose to intervene at each step, cool down, and break the pattern – or he can continue down his destructive path.

1. Don't say 'should'

The first and most important step consists of breaking the 'should' rule.

Much of Peter's life is governed by such rules. He has rules and expectations for his own behaviour and for others' behaviour – he even feels the weight of other's rules on him. He has more rules than a legal tome. The result? – Anger, guilt, and intense pressure to live up to his standards.

But he cannot live up to such unrelenting standards, and neither can others. Peter makes many demands. 'People should listen to me.' 'They should stay out of the way.' 'I should have total control over this situation.' But the fact of the matter is that people don't listen, they do get in his way, and he cannot control their behaviour. At this point, Peter has the choice of accepting the circumstances that have arisen or of hammering away against reality, demanding that it should not be that way. He has an option of challenging the 'should' style of thinking that is causing him to get so angry.

What else could Peter say instead of the thoughts above? Cover the rest of the page and write a short script for Peter. Then take a peek and see if you are thinking along the right lines.

Possible script for Peter

_____

_____

Here's our suggestion:

'Realistically people do ignore my wishes and intrude. What, constructively, can I do when that happens? I can continue to follow my own 'rules', to treat others fairly and well, but not to insist that they respond to me in the same way. It would be nice if they did, but if they don't, they don't. Tough! Too bad!'

TOP TIP

♦ Rigid thinking, with lots of 'shoulds' in it will ensure that we get high blood pressure very quickly when others fail to respond to our rules. Learn to be more flexible.

Activity
Re-write your own rules

● Do you have 'should' rules for how others should behave? Write a few of them down. For example, 'People should not drop litter in the street.'

● Now re-write these sentences without using the word should.

OVERCOMING STRESS-RELATED ANGER

More tools to use

Coming to terms with the concept that others might very well not follow our own ideas about behaviour is a good start.

> **Today you will learn ...**
>
> tools for reducing angry thoughts and feelings.

2. What's really upsetting you?

The second step is to examine what really hurts when one of our rules is broken. For example, when Peter is angry and hurt, he can ask himself, 'What really hurts here?' Maybe he thinks, 'People are rude and insensitive,' 'I'll be made the victim,' or 'I'm powerless to do anything about this.'

What hurts Peter the most is his inability to change people's behaviour.

What could he say instead of the thoughts above? As you did yesterday, cover the rest of the page and write a short script for Peter. Then check your suggestions against ours.

Possible script for Peter

_____

_____

_____

_____

_____

_____

_____

_____

Here's our suggestion:

'There is no evidence that I should be able to control people. They are responsible for their own beliefs, behaviours, attitudes and assumptions. Perhaps I can see myself not as a victim, but as a person who can choose how to be.'

3. Keep your cool!

Respond to hot, anger-driven thoughts with cooler, more level-headed thoughts. Peter initially thinks, 'How dare he?' but he can replace that thought with, 'He thinks he is trying to help me.' Peter thinks, 'How stupid can she be?' but he can instead respond, 'She's human.'

> **TOP TIP**
>
> ♦ To reduce your anger, change your script.

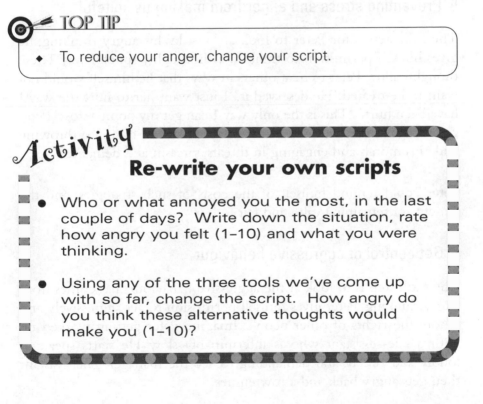

ℐctivity

Re-write your own scripts

● Who or what annoyed you the most, in the last couple of days? Write down the situation, rate how angry you felt (1–10) and what you were thinking.

● Using any of the three tools we've come up with so far, change the script. How angry do you think these alternative thoughts would make you (1–10)?

OVERCOMING STRESS-RELATED ANGER

Even more tools to use

4. Using relaxation skills

The next step is to respond to the angry feelings themselves. Peter can do this by practising relaxation and deep breathing. He can relax his muscles, and re-focus his attention away from the stressful situation.

> **Today you will learn ...**
>
> to relax, not to be spiteful, to get control of aggressive behaviour.

The relaxation and breathing skills you have hopefully mastered should now come into their own.

5. Preventing stress and anger from making us spiteful

The fifth step is for Peter to look at how, by his angry thinking, he gives himself permission to think in a thoroughly spiteful way. These thoughts allow Peter to treat others in ways that he himself would not want to be treated. 'He deserved it.' 'I just want her to hurt the way I have been hurt.' 'This is the only way I can get my point across.' Peter can recognise these ideas as 'con artistry.' They con him into throwing aside his morals and engaging in threats, sarcasm and demands.

Peter could remind himself of the costs of such strategies, and the benefits of remaining calm and fair.

6. Get control of aggressive behaviour

The sixth step is to look at the aggressive behaviour that comes from angry thinking. Peter gives himself permission to act aggressively and ignore the rights of other people. Imagine Peter getting worked up with a sales assistant who is interminably slow. He starts speaking loudly and rudely, and demanding to see the manager. The assistant then gets angry back and a row ensues.

What other choices does Peter have?

- He could attempt to understand the cause of the assistant's slowness.
- He could put himself in the other person's shoes, imagine what he is thinking and feeling, and attempt to understand his point of view.
- He could ask himself how important this delay really is?

This will help to:

- Decrease Peter's anger
- Decrease the other person's anger
- Increase the likelihood that the other person will hear what Peter has to say
- Increase the likelihood of the two of them having a rational and reasonable conversation.

TOP TIP

- Keep up with deep breathing and relaxation practice to help you when you feel your anger rising.
- Don't give yourself permission to think spiteful thoughts.
- Don't let aggressive behaviour control you.

Activity

Relax!

- Do a few relaxation exercises. If you are out of practice, go back and reread Days 41–48 and pick out a few favourites to use.

OVERCOMING STRESS-RELATED ANGER

Learning to own your anger

One of the difficulties we can have in keeping calm in provoking situations is the idea that none of this is our fault. If the other person had not done this, that or the other, we would never have reacted in that way. So it was their fault.

> **Today you will learn ...**
>
> who is responsible for your
> anger, and why.

This may be partially true. Someone may well have been extremely thoughtless, careless or acted stupidly. You may well be the victim of their rotten judgement. However, the other person is responsible for their actions – but you are responsible for your response.

CASE STUDY

Sally had been having a terrible day. Things were going badly at work and she was under a lot of stress. She had social plans for the evening, but the work tasks kept rolling onto her desk, and they were all marked 'urgent'. Finally, Sally felt that she had things well enough under control to shut down her computer and head for the door. Looking at her watch, Sally saw that she had just enough time to make her appointment and not be late, provided she had a good journey home, and no hold-ups. Sally walked quickly to her car – where she noticed, to her absolute horror, that a delivery truck was parked right across her bay, denying her access out. Sally just could not believe it. She felt anger rise up within her. Her heart started beating fast and a hot rush of emotion welled up inside her. Looking round, she saw the probable driver of the vehicle standing chatting with another man further up the car park. This added to Sally's anger. 'How dare he?' she thought. 'Not only has he blocked my space, but he has no sense of urgency about rectifying the situation.' Sally rushed up to the driver, and started shouting at him. 'You selfish idiot. Can't you see you have blocked me in. I'm going to miss a theatre date because of your selfishness.' 'Keep your hair on,' was the response Sally got. 'No need to get so uptight about it. I'll be there in a minute.' Sally went through the roof! This was so unjust, so unfair, and she simply 'lost it' at the outrageous way she perceived the driver to be behaving. She starting screaming at him at the top of her voice, and even swung her briefcase towards him, hitting him on the leg. He moved to defend himself and the bystander had to restrain Sally, who ended up so distraught she had to be taken back to her office reception area to calm down. Needless to say, she never made the theatre.

Who do you consider was to blame for Sally's anger and distress?

- The lorry driver was to blame.
- The other man contributed.
- The overall unfortunate circumstances were the problem.
- Sally was the culprit.

The answer is Sally, by 100%.

The truck driver was to blame for:

- Thoughtless parking
- Time-wasting when he should have been delivering his goods
- Total insensitivity to Sally's predicament
- His rude response when she pointed it out to him.

But Sally was to blame for allowing herself to become so angry that she lost control of the situation.

TOP TIP

- You are the owner of your anger – you are the decision-maker as to when and to what extent you use this emotion. No one else decides this for you. People sometimes work very hard to provoke you – nonetheless, you control, and therefore decide upon, your reactions.

Activity
Who made you angry?

- Think of the last time you felt really angry. What was the story behind it? Who did you feel made you angry? If the answer is 'The person who ...' take another look at the case study. Now answer that question again.

- Who made you angry?

Defuse stress with humour

Right. You finally decide on the new bookcase you want for your lounge. Seeing that it is much cheaper to DIY, you purchase the 'flat–pack' version. However, when you get it home, you discover that the instructions were

> **Today you will learn ...**
>
> that humour is a great de-stressor.

written by someone for whom English is definitely not their first language – and all the nuts and bolts look the same. It takes you the best part of a day to put up, despite 'Easy to assemble' printed all over the packaging – and when you start to load your book collection into it, the whole unit falls apart.

Now answer the following questions.

1 How do you react? Do you:
   ◆ Fume
   ◆ Cry
   ◆ Have a laugh
   Answer: Be totally honest about this. We suspect that if you are, most of you will have admitted to the first or second options.

2 What difference to the final outcome do any of these responses make?
   Answer: Zero.

3 With that in mind, which of the above responses is likely to relieve your stress most?
   Answer: Almost certainly, laughing.

We know, we know – it's not at all funny and it is very frustrating ('I spent all day ... blah, blah, blah ...').

4 If someone else told you this story in the pub or at a supper party, how would you respond?
   Answer: We bet you'd laugh.

OVERCOMING STRESS-RELATED ANGER

So what do you make of all this? Is it that:

◆ It's funny when it happens to someone else, but not when it happens to me.
◆ It's hard to see the funny side of such things at the time.
◆ I don't actively look for the funny side of things.
◆ It's childish to use humour when something goes wrong.

Or, just possibly:

◆ Perhaps I need to cultivate using humour more as an alternative to getting worked up, angry, and stressed out.

TOP TIP

◆ Seeing the funny side of things is less stressful than getting angry.

If you think this might be the case, turn the page. Over the next two days we will look at the many benefits of using humour – and how to make it your first option, rather than a last resort.

Activity

Could you use humour?

When did you last laugh at yourself? What happened?

● Look through your notes for one or two stressful situations. (You will have a great many of them logged in by now, so we won't ask you to find even more!)

● Re-think the situation – could you have used humour? If you told the tale to a friend at a later stage, would it have sounded humorous?

OVERCOMING STRESS-RELATED ANGER

Laugh to improve your health

Almost all of us feel better when we have a laugh. However, you may not be aware of quite what a good stress-buster laughter is – which is why we are spending some time and effort on it in this book.

> **Today you will learn ...**
>
> what you actually already know – that laughter is the best medicine.

Can you think of any ways that laughing might help you physically? Cover the rest of the page, and then jot your ideas down below.

1 _____

2 _____

3 _____

You have already learned a great deal in this book about the importance of relaxation. Laughter is a very natural way of achieving this. Following a good laugh, generally your blood pressure will drop and your heart rate slow down. You will breathe more deeply and feel a great deal calmer. Totally worthwhile.

Here are some good ways in which humor can lower stress. Did you come up with any of these yourself?

◆ Humour stops you getting even more worked up.
  You now understand the anger spiral – stress begets stress, and on it goes, until we explode or implode. So even if you start off by getting distressed (that bookshelf falling down was quite a dreadful event to happen!) you can stop the spiral going ever upward by 'breaking' the situation with humour.
◆ You strengthen your immune system.
  More laughter equals less stress, equals less harmful stress hormones circulating round your body. That must be good.

◆ Laughter is infectious and habit-forming.

'Practising laughing' is no different from practising anything else. The more you do it, the easier and more quickly it will become a natural 'first resort'. So even though it might not be your normal first response, try to begin to look for the funny side of things (use today's activity to practise this).

◆ Laughing at yourself stops you winding yourself up.

Remember how we looked at the way stress increases according to the importance we give to a situation going wrong? Well, it's just the same when we ourselves 'go wrong'. Often, we take ourselves too seriously – we look for perfection and get stressed when we fail to achieve it. Learn to laugh at your errors and cock-ups instead. Not only will you see that things matter a lot less than you thought – you will give others the chance to share a joke as well.

TOP TIP

◆ Laughter is very good for you physically as well as emotionally.
◆ Learn to 'practise' seeing the funny side of life, so that it becomes more natural to do so.

Activity
Find the funny side

● Look back over the last two weeks. Write down the situations that stressed you out the most (three or four, if you can).

● Now suppose you were asked to see a funny side to what happened, or to your reaction to what happened. Could you?

● Write your suggestions down.

This is one of the many activities that you really need to keep practising. Unless you are already the comic of your family or the office (in which case, stress may not trouble you much) it will take a while to 'loosen up' naturally.

OVERCOMING STRESS-RELATED ANGER

Making humour your first option

How you 'practise laughing' is really no different from practising anything else. Use today's activity to start you off. Begin by writing down situations where everything has gone wrong. Then ask yourself two questions:

> **Today you will learn ...**
>
> how to find the funny side.

1 Was there anything at all humorous in this situation?

  For example, you have spent the day deliberately trying not to hear the football results before you get to watch *Match of the Day*, only to have your eight-year-old son tell you the result just as you sit down to watch it. You could go through the roof, or sigh with despair. However, it is also quite a funny story.

2 Could I perhaps have looked at events more light-heartedly?

  For example, you are running desperately to catch a bus, knowing that if you miss it you will have to wait half an hour for the next one. As you reach it, you slip on a dog turd, your scarf gets caught on a hedge and starts strangling you, and when you reach out to steady yourself, you grab someone else who falls over with you. No one is hurt, and the person you pull over is smiling at the ridiculous train of events – but you don't catch the bus.

  Is this a funny story or a horror story? If you see it as a funny story – and more importantly, did so at the time that it happened – your stress levels will be a lot lower.

An extra suggestion – watch more 'stand-up' comedians.

Yes, really! (If you are a satellite subscriber, you will find them on the comedy channels.) These people make the most dire situations sound hilarious, and the more you listen, the more you will learn how to do the same. Then 'get out there' and start practising!

We are not suggesting that **all** situations can boast a humorous side, and we appreciate that many don't. Here are two specific instances when laughter is **not** the right response.

1 Inappropriate laughter.
   This usually involves not laughing at other people's misfortunes, or when a mess-up has caused a serious or harmful result, or when it is obvious that everyone else is taking whatever it is very seriously. Hopefully, your instincts will tell you when laughter is inappropriate. If not, then spend some time learning to apologise well.

2 Malicious laughter.
   We hope you will know exactly what we mean here. If you had red hair or glasses at school, you may understand entirely how horrendous malicious laughter is. Poking fun at others to raise a laugh, telling stories that show others up in a poor light, hooting when someone spills burning coffee on themselves – these are not ways to make friends, or to reduce your stress levels. Only use this type of laughter on yourself.

TOP TIP

- Find the humorous side of a situation as a first, rather than a last resort.
- Laughter isn't always appropriate – use discretion.

Activity

Hone your sense of humour

Use the back of your notebook to start a stress/humour list.

- Simply draw a line down the middle of the page.
- On one side write down the latest stressful incident, and on the other side, write down any comic elements (look back at the above examples if you are struggling).

Do this at least twice a week for two months – or until it becomes more natural for you to see the funny side of things more easily.

OVERCOMING STRESS-RELATED ANGER

Are you keeping up? Do you need some help? If you've not already subscribed, why not try the daily text messaging service for extra encouragement and support. Just text 'Mellow 71' to 80881 now.

Each set of messages costs £1.50. Please see page xii for full terms and conditions.

Some final points on anger

You are now becoming expert at managing anger. However, before we move on, here are just a few more points that we believe will assist you.

> **Today you will learn ...**
>
> a few, final, miscellaneous ways to reduce anger.

'Letting it all out' – isn't this healthier than keeping it bottled up? Well, yes and no. Think about people you know who constantly vent their anger. Don't they simply seem 'angry all the time'? Aren't they the sort of people you avoid confrontations with if you can? Releasing your anger can actually become just as much of a habit as anything else. You will get used to exploding, and react instinctively in a hostile way. 'Letting it all out' is not going to reduce your anger habit at all.

Equally, neither is bottling it up. Fuming internally whilst saying nothing is not at all healthy. The key is to 're-package' what you want to express in a healthier and less confrontational way.

Such unhelpful strategies are likely to increase your blood pressure.

Strategies for keeping calm

This is a variation on the work you have done previously on challenging negative or unhelpful thoughts. When you feel yourself getting worked up, instead of feeding the anger by saying to yourself 'That guy's an idiot', 'This queue is never going to move', use calming self-suggestions instead. A few examples might be:

- Is this really worth getting worked up about?
- Does getting angry help the situation?
- Other people can do what they wish.
- I'm not going to take this personally.
- I don't **have** to get angry. It's my choice.
- The guy is fallible just like the rest of us.
- I'm living proof that I can stand queuing.
- I'll take some deep breaths and stay calm.

Think up some calming thoughts of your own (see today's activity). The important strategy is to find a statement to say to yourself that will reduce your anger rather than increase it.

Rehearsing situations

Sometimes, we find ourselves getting wound up again and again by the same old stuff. How futile is that? So, if you know a situation is coming up that normally is irritating – for example, the meaningless team meetings you have to sit through every Monday – rehearse ahead of time what you can do to reduce or eliminate this annoyance, rather than simply accepting it as a fact of life.

Counting to ten

This is such an old adage, but it can often work. 'Counting to ten' might mean leaving the situation for a while, distracting yourself for a time and returning to your angry thoughts after a break to see if they have reduced – or it might literally mean counting to ten. In any event, pausing mentally before 'going in' can be a helpful way of calming down.

TOP TIP

- Venting anger is not usually a good idea. Learn to re-package your messages in a less hostile way.
- Have a stock of calming statements to defuse angry thinking.
- Don't keep getting angry about the same old things.
- Count to ten!

Activity Calming comments

- Go to the back of your diary. Starting a new sheet, head it 'Calming self-talk for angry situations'.
- Write down at least six sentences that you feel would work for you.

Add to this list regularly, so that you build up a good stock of helpful challenges to your angry thoughts.

OVERCOMING STRESS-RELATED ANGER

Your notes

CHAPTER 8

IMPROVE YOUR COMMUNICATION SKILLS

How not to let others wind you up

> **Today you will learn ...**
>
> that is it easier to deal with difficult people and situations if we improve our own communication skills.

Do you ever feel that it is really not you, it is everybody else, who is difficult, rude and obstructive? Do other people cause most of the stress in your life? These others may be your family, they may be your work colleagues, they may simply be irritating 'types' – those, for example who chat away to shop assistants, unaware that the queue behind them grows longer and longer as they do so. You are not alone!

However, as you have already learned, it is a hard task to change the attitudes and behaviours of others – all we can try to do is to influence them. Getting stressed about it is even more exhausting. Learning to improve your own communication skills is a positive way forward.

Think about the reasons for communication:

◆ To pass on information
◆ To ask for what we want
◆ To share how we feel
◆ To understand how others feel
◆ To achieve goals and outcomes.

Getting what we want is a huge benefit of communicating well. But as well as this, we are more likely to command the respect of others, and we are usually happier about ourselves (= more relaxed, = less stressed).

◎ TOP TIP

> ◆ If we learn to communicate really well, we are more likely to get what we want.

IMPROVE YOUR COMMUNICATION SKILLS

One key feature of communicating well is to ensure that people understand the point we are making. Too often, we simply assume that they do. Here are some wonderful examples, from a variety of locations, of typical communication errors.

After making tea, staff should empty tea pot and stand upside down on draining board.	Would the person who took the step ladder please return it immediately or further steps will be taken.
Automatic washing machines: please remove all your clothes when red light goes out.	Toilet out of order: please use floor below.

⊙ TOP TIP

♦ Whilst you may believe that other people wind you up, improving your own communication skills can get you closer to the results you want.

Activity
How well do you communicate?

● Think back over the last week. Either at home or at work, you will probably have had at least one difficult conversation. How well do you think it went? Did it get you the result you wanted? If not, why not? Did you feel frustrated at the end of it?

● Or perhaps you can recall handling a difficult conversation well. What did you do that resulted in a favourable outcome?

IMPROVE YOUR COMMUNICATION SKILLS

Listening skills

Communication is not just about talking. It is about listening and understanding.

> **Today you will learn ...**
>
> the importance of listening.

One reason for failing to relate well to others is that we become very self-focused in conversations. We are often either talking or waiting. In other words – when we are not speaking ourselves, we are simply preparing for the next opportunity to speak, rather than actively listening to the other person, and showing them that we understand what they are saying.

Listening skills

Listening skills are very important. Develop them if you are a poor listener as otherwise life will be more stressful. People won't relate to you well, and your personal and work relationships will almost certainly not be as good as they could be. Good listeners tend to have less stress in their lives as they, quite simply, get on better with people.

Choose the right time

In order to be a good listener, you will benefit from being in the right frame of mind. You also need to be sure that this is a good time for the person who needs to speak to you. Do they want to talk to you now? Would later be better? Become aware of your own needs and feelings. Will you focus better when you have made that urgent phone call? It is important to be able to give others the time they need to express themselves, so timing can be of crucial importance.

Be an active listener

We have all experienced, at some point or another, telling somebody something important and getting little or no response. This didn't necessarily mean that they were not listening – but it might have done! Being active in your listening involves indicating to the other person that you are focusing on what they have to say. You can do this by:

- Saying 'I see,' 'I understand,' 'Go on,' etc – short phrases that indicate that you are 'with' the other person
- Using facial expressions to reflect what it being said – a smile, a frown, a nod, are all powerful indicators that you are listening closely
- If you are not certain what exactly has been said – say so. 'I'm not sure what you mean by that.' 'When did this happen exactly?' 'Were you angry or disappointed?'

Acknowledge understanding with feedback

We usually feel most heard when someone reflects back to us what we have just said. For example: 'It sounds as though you are really struggling at present. Tom's away a great deal, and with three children under five, it is often too much to cope with on your own.' The relief of being able to say, 'Yes, that's exactly how it is,' and knowing that you have been listened to and understood, creates great respect and closeness between two people.

Understanding is enabling

A further important advantage of understanding the other person's point of view is that they will almost certainly be far more receptive to hearing yours in due course.

TOP TIP

- Communicating well involves listening and understanding as well as talking.

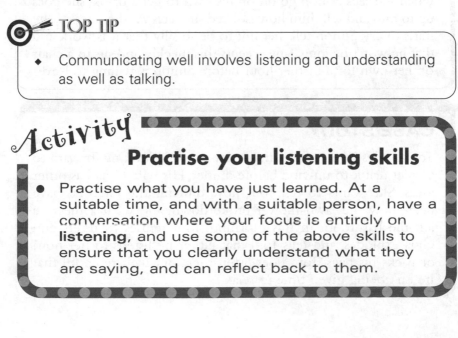

Activity

Practise your listening skills

- Practise what you have just learned. At a suitable time, and with a suitable person, have a conversation where your focus is entirely on **listening**, and use some of the above skills to ensure that you clearly understand what they are saying, and can reflect back to them.

IMPROVE YOUR COMMUNICATION SKILLS

What is your personal talking style?

> **Today you will learn ...**
>
> it's not what you say, it's the way that you say it.

What you say, and how you say it, will decide whether you achieve a good outcome, or feel more stressed than ever when the conversation ends.

What is your personal style? Do you tend to be:

◆ Passive ('Oh, all right then.')
◆ Aggressive ('Because I say so, that's why.')
◆ Assertive ('I'd like to help, but I'm too busy right now.').

Look at these examples.

CASE STUDY

Jane and Simon go to Simon's office party together. However, soon after they arrive, Simon drifts off and starts chatting to people that Jane doesn't know. He does not introduce her, but leaves her to her own devices. Jane does not like to interrupt, but when she sees Simon go off on his own to get a drink, she goes up to him and tells him how isolated she feels. As she does so, she starts to cry. Simon tells her not to be so silly, that it is work and that he won't be long. Jane accepts this meekly, and sits in a chair on her own for a further hour before Simon is willing to leave.

CASE STUDY

Tom comes home after a tiring day at work, looking forward to a quiet drink to unwind before dinner. His wife Gina has other ideas. She wants to tell Tom how difficult the children have been, how the lawn-mower broke down, and what a mess he left the bathroom in this morning. Tom refuses to listen, and Gina explodes, and tells Tom that either he listens to her now, or packs his bags. Tom does listen then, but feels resentful that he isn't being given time to relax.

IMPROVE YOUR COMMUNICATION SKILLS

CASE STUDY

Lisa's boss asks her to stay late at work on a night that she has theatre tickets. When she tells him this, he says, 'But this is vital. It is for a meeting at 9 am tomorrow for a most important client.' Lisa responds, 'I'm really sorry. I appreciate how important it is, but I cannot stay late tonight. If it helps, I would be happy to come in early tomorrow morning, to ensure that you have the work before 9 am.' Her boss, in turn, thanks her for her understanding, and when she comes in early the next morning, there is a small box of chocolates on her desk as a 'thank you'.

No prizes for guessing who is passive (Jane), aggressive (Gina) and assertive (Lisa).

The question is, simply – who gets the best outcome?

TOP TIP

- ◆ The three main communication styles are Passive, Aggressive and Assertive. You will probably use all three communication skills from time to time, but learning to focus on being assertive will get you the best relationship results.

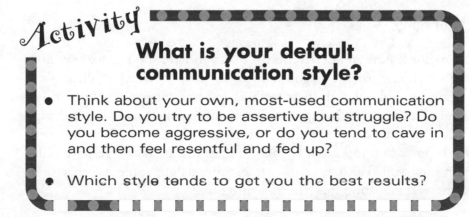

Activity **What is your default communication style?**

- ● Think about your own, most-used communication style. Do you try to be assertive but struggle? Do you become aggressive, or do you tend to cave in and then feel resentful and fed up?

- ● Which style tends to get you the best results?

IMPROVE YOUR COMMUNICATION SKILLS

Focusing on assertiveness skills

Unless you are aggressive and enjoy it (it does get instant results, but usually at the expense of longer term relationships) or cave in and prefer a peaceful life, you will find that the more assertive you become, the happier you will be and the less stress you will feel at the outcome.

> **Today you will learn ...**
>
> the strengths of assertive behaviour in helping you communicate well and achieve your goals.

Features of an assertive communication style

◆ Keen to find a solution to problems where everyone is satisfied
◆ Strong enough to stand up calmly for your own rights
◆ Able to accept without rancour that others have rights too
◆ Interested in the other person's point of view.

Two major reasons for choosing to negotiate assertively are:

◆ It is usually effective. You are more likely to get the outcome you want.
◆ It is the style that others appreciate the most. Therefore, they are less likely to avoid negotiating with you, as they can rely on your remaining calm and looking for a good outcome for both of you.

Your rights

A major feature of assertiveness is that you have the right to say how you feel. The passive person fails to say how they feel at all, and the aggressor will not own their feelings, but will suggest that you 'made' them feel that way. Being assertive means saying 'I feel very unhappy when you speak to me like that,' rather than 'You make me very unhappy when you speak to me like that.' You are taking responsibility for how you feel but, at the same time, telling someone that their actions are creating these feelings in you.

Standing your ground

Staying calm and standing firm at the same time takes a lot of practice, but is well worth the effort. In order to do this, you need to keep things simple, and operate on a three-step basis.

The three steps are as follows:

1 Acknowledge, for example, 'I appreciate this project is important'.
2 Use 'however' to state how you feel, for example, 'However I need to leave work promptly at five o'clock today'.
3 Offer an alternative solution where you can, for example, 'I can still finish the project by ten o'clock tomorrow morning, if I start by eight thirty tomorrow'.

We are only briefly touching on the various skills that will help you develop your assertiveness. You may wish to read further books devoted entirely to this topic.

TOP TIP

♦ Standing your ground can be done in a calm and understanding way that means you do not need to 'give way' – and yet the other person will also feel that they have achieved a result.

Activity
Practise being assertive

A fun way to practise assertiveness skills is to role play.

● Perhaps you have a friend, partner or work colleague who might do this with you? You need your partner to be as tricky as possible, whilst you practise the techniques we have outlined above. (Avoid arguing.)

● Then let them use the same skills on you.

IMPROVE YOUR COMMUNICATION SKILLS

Avoid being manipulated

Basic assertiveness skills will take you a long way – but some of those you interact with will be experts in manipulation. Dealing with people who are determined to get their own way can be stressful, especially if this happens on a daily basis.

> **Today you will learn ...**
>
> skills to prevent others getting the better of you.

Today, you will look at a few of the ways people can attempt to get the better of you, and how you can specifically counter-punch to stay in the winner's corner.

Broken record technique

When people try to push you around, use the Broken Record Technique. This consists of sticking with the 3-step skill we mentioned yesterday, and simply repeating the same clear, simple points in the face of continued argument. You do not need to widen your own argument – simply acknowledge/state your view/offer a solution again and again in a firm but calm way until the other person backs down.

Keep a narrow focus

Don't allow other people to widen the argument. One moment they are talking about your forgetting to put the rubbish out this morning, and the next minute they seem to be talking about every failing you have had over the last five years. Draw the discussion back to the specific instance: 'For the moment, let's just talk about what is upsetting you right now.' 'I don't necessarily disagree with your points, but let's focus on the present problem.'

Laugh about it

When someone keeps plugging away at a perceived weakness – for example, 'Your spelling is atrocious. There are six errors on the first page alone of this proposal.' – a defusing response might be, 'Six errors – my apologies. Let me take it back to correct and I'll give my spellchecker a detention for hopeless work!'

IMPROVE YOUR COMMUNICATION SKILLS

Ignore the tears

Don't allow others to play the victim. Acknowledge the emotion with, 'I can see this is upsetting you, however …' then assertively and clearly stay with your point.

Interested enquiry

If someone is critical of something that you have done, instead of defending yourself, come right back with something like, 'Exactly what **was** it about my cleaning the lounge that you believed wasn't good enough?' Don't take offence – simply take an interested stance on the issue, focusing on your behaviour only.

Delaying

You do not need to respond immediately to comments or criticisms, which may lead you to use words you wish you had not, and vice versa. Say, 'I'll get back to you on those points when I've had more time to think about them / obtained further information / talked to Jo Bloggs.' This will give you time to calm down and collect your thoughts.

TOP TIP

◆ The more you use these assertion skills the easier they become and the more relaxed you will feel about dealing with difficult situations. Dread will be replaced by confidence.

Activity
Put assertiveness into practice

● Earmark someone you have to deal with regularly, who can be quite difficult.

● Decide ahead of time which of the above skills would be appropriate to use, and when you get the opportunity, give them a go. Make a note of any difference it makes.

IMPROVE YOUR COMMUNICATION SKILLS

Dealing with threats and abuse

Living with, or working with, others who use aggression in order to get their own way can be very stressful indeed if you do not know how to deal with it. So learning how to defuse another person's threatening or abusive behaviour is an obviously important skill.

> **Today you will learn ...**
>
> how to defuse abusive behaviour from others.

You need to have started developing assertiveness skills before you can deal with this. If you have not yet mastered your own behaviour, you cannot expect others to have mastered theirs.

You can walk away

When you are truly being unfairly attacked you can stand up for yourself. If you are uncertain that you will be able to control either your reaction or the situation, then take yourself out of the situation if you possibly can.

Positive self-talk

Then calm yourself down. Maintaining internal hurt, fear or anger will do you no good, so talk yourself through it.

- Jim tends to fly off the handle easily with everyone.
- I'll take some deep breaths and relax.
- Why should I let someone else's behaviour affect my own?
- Being treated unfairly is a fact of life. I will get over it.
- Retaliation certainly won't help.

By taking this action, you are defusing your own anger.

Acknowledge the abusive behaviour

Where you need to stand your ground, don't initially attempt any defence of what is being said to you. To defuse the situation and avoid further confrontation, acknowledging the other person's view (however outrageous and irrational) is a strong response, not a weak one.

'You sound outraged by what has happened,' for example, may take the wind out of their sails. Bearing in mind that your goal is to calm the other person down, this is an important start.

Be honest about how you feel

If someone is treating you aggressively – especially in a work or domestic situation – tell them clearly how you are feeling. 'I feel quite frightened when you react like that,' 'While you are so angry, I don't feel able to talk to you.' These are all valid observations that you have a right to make, and will encourage the abuser to take stock of their own behaviour.

Offer an apology (a backstop)

If you are really in fear of someone's violent temper, then holding out an olive branch may be a better solution than ending up with a black eye. This can be more a statement of regret – for example, 'I'm really sorry that what I have done has caused you to get so angry.' These are not weak responses in these circumstances. They are conciliatory responses that may defuse the situation.

Agree!

What is actually more 'show stopping' than being calmly agreed with when you get very worked up with and critical about someone? 'You're quite right. I did forget to pay the gas bill.'

 TOP TIP

♦ When confronted with real abuse or threatening behaviour, your goal is to defuse the situation and to remain safe.

Activity

How well do you handle conflict?

● Can you recall the last time you felt threatened or abused by someone's behaviour? How did you react? Were you able to use any skills to defuse the situation?

IMPROVE YOUR COMMUNICATION SKILLS

Don't take it personally

One of the reasons that dealing with others can be particularly stressful is that we can take comments and criticisms very personally. For example, if a shop assistant is rude to you, you might believe that a) she has taken a dislike to you, or b) you have done something to upset her.

> **Today you will learn ...**
>
> that dealing with other people who are stressed or upset can be hard enough. Don't make it worse by personalising it.

How do you feel if a friend says she will call you and does not? Or if someone simply disagrees with a point you are making? These situations are upsetting – we want our friends to call us, and for people to agree with our opinions. However, any stress that we feel when such things happen will be greatly magnified if we decide that the reason it has happened is due to our own failings or shortcomings.

Personalisation

Personalisation means that you erroneously feel that you are personally to blame for the perceived negative reactions of others. 'If someone disagrees with me, then I must be wrong, and that makes me stupid.' What a very stress–provoking thought that is!

De-personalisation

De-personalising involves using some of the broader thinking skills you learned about earlier in this book.

◆ Have respect for the opinions of others. There is no rule that says everyone must agree with you, or that if they don't, you are stupid.
◆ Distinguish between opinion and fact. However strongly either you, or the person talking to you, believes something, that doesn't make it true. There are many different opinions on almost every subject. Opinions are exactly that – simply points of view.
◆ Have confidence in your own views. You don't need to be right all the time – simply having a view shows some thoughtful

intelligence on your part, and you may have valid reasons / past experiences that mean you are more likely to have formed your opinions in a certain way.

◆ Others have their own problems. The rude shop assistant may have had a row with her boyfriend.

◆ Other people suffer from stress as well, and don't always react in the best possible way. This has nothing to do with you.

Use the cricket ball technique

One of the authors of this book worked with a client who was personalising every criticism his wife made, and it was affecting their relationship very badly. He was a cricket fan, and one day, he came into the office and said:

'I can see that personalising criticism is like letting a cricket ball hit me on the head. It hurts a great deal and leaves a big bump. I now know that I can hold my hand up and catch the ball [the personal criticism] before it hits me. I can then choose what to do with it. I can look at it, play with it, put it down, or even throw it back. But I don't need to let it hit me on the head and hurt me.'

◎ TOP TIP

◆ Altercations or criticism can be very stressful. Don't make the stress even worse by attributing the other person's anger to your personal failings.

Activity De-personalisation

● Think back over the last week. Can you identify an occasion when you might have erroneously taken something too personally? What went through your mind? Using your notebook, jot down some alternative ways of thinking about this.

● How do you feel now?

IMPROVE YOUR COMMUNICATION SKILLS

Communication without words

Today you will learn ...

how much you learn from (or give away to) others without saying a word ...

Various studies have shown that the words we speak have far less impact than our tone of voice or our body language.

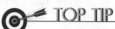

TOP TIP

- Just 7% of our communication comes from the words we speak.
- 38% comes from our tone of voice.
- 55% comes from our body language.

If you find that hard to believe, here is a question for you to think about. How would you know, without that person saying a word, if they were:

- Sad?
- Happy?
- Angry?
- Bored?
- Arrogant?
- Interested?
- Disinterested?
- Pleased?

How much is it possible to learn about someone's frame of mind without them actually saying anything? In turn, even when you do not say a word, you are telling people a great deal about what is in your mind! Picture this:

You walk into a large restaurant, looking for a friend. In the distance you see a couple leaning towards each other across a table. They are speaking, but you cannot hear them. Yet you can (usually) easily tell if the couple are a) being intimate b) arguing c) sharing a joke d) discussing a serious matter.

All this, without hearing a word they are saying. Bear that in mind.

Now think about your own body language and tone of voice.

You are at a party that you were quite nervous about going to. Lots of elegant people will be there, and you don't know anyone except the host and one or two others. You need to start up some conversations and get to know a few people. You pick someone to initially approach and chat to.

Now list five things you might do that are non-verbal that would a) show warmth and interest and b) show coolness and disinterest.

1 _____   1 _____
2 _____   2 _____
3 _____   3 _____
4 _____   4 _____
5 _____   5 _____

The crucial thing is to ensure that your body language and your tone **match** what you are saying, as your non-verbal communication will give a stronger message than your verbal communication. For example, inviting someone to lunch whilst continuing to work on your computer will not convey great enthusiasm for the idea.

TOP TIP

♦ How you communicate through body language and tone of voice gives a far stronger message than the words you are saying.

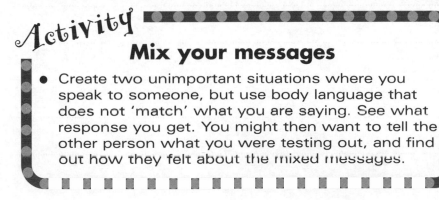

Activity

Mix your messages

● Create two unimportant situations where you speak to someone, but use body language that does not 'match' what you are saying. See what response you get. You might then want to tell the other person what you were testing out, and find out how they felt about the mixed messages.

IMPROVE YOUR COMMUNICATION SKILLS

Your notes

CHAPTER 9

**STRESS AT WORK,
STRESS AT HOME**

Recognising stress at work

We discussed earlier on the difference between pressure – which is actually good for us – and stress, which is bad for us. In a working environment where, usually, we do not have full control, it is important to recognise any movement from pressure to stress.

> **Today you will learn ...**
>
> to assess your stress levels in the workplace and identify your personal stress triggers.

We are expected to put up with a certain amount of pressure, and are capable of doing so, but if we find ourselves heading towards job burnout, action needs to be taken. The following can be causes of burnout. Do any apply to you?

- ◆ Work overload – you have more to do that you can cope with, and/or deadlines that you find impossible to meet.
- ◆ Work underload – you do not have enough to do, and your job is boring.
- ◆ Your work is not recognised/ rewarded.
- ◆ You are not given the skills to do the job.
- ◆ You work with uncooperative colleagues.
- ◆ You are a victim of bullying or harassment.
- ◆ You have lack of control over your job that leads to frustration.

Are you coping? First, you need to identify the symptoms that indicate stress.

◎✎ TOP TIP

- ◆ Workplace stress is a serious issue. You need to identify it before it causes you to become physically ill and unable to work.

Tick the statement that apply to you:
- Is your concentration poorer than in the past? ☐
- Do you feel tired all the time? ☐
- Has your enthusiasm for your job waned? ☐
- Does getting up to go to work make you feel depressed? ☐
- Do you long for weekends/holidays? ☐
- Do you see your job simply as a means of paying the bills? ☐
- Are you concerned with your on-the-job performance? ☐
- Are you relating poorly to your boss? ☐
- Are you eating or drinking more or less than usual? ☐
- Have you lost interest in your social life? ☐

As few as three ticks should concern you.

Of the following statements, tick those that make you feel stressed and rate them in order of priority (10 = this stresses me the most).

Rating
- Do you feel that you have far too much to do? ☐ ____
- Do you feel that you have too little to do? ☐ ____
- Do you feel you have too much responsibility? ☐ ____
- Do you feel that you lack authority? ☐ ____
- Do you work hours far in excess of those in your job spec? ☐ ____
- Do you find your boss/colleagues difficult to get on with, or unhelpful? ☐ ____
- Do you feel criticised rather than appreciated? ☐ ____
- Do you feel that there is no relationship between your hard work and the rewards you receive in terms of recognition and salary? ☐ ____
- Do you feel unable to perform to your best abilities because of the amount of work you must get through? ☐ ____
- Do you feel less and less able to cope? ☐ ____

You should have now identified a) whether you are suffering from job stress or burnout, and b) which stress triggers affect you the most.

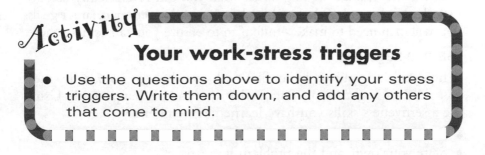

Activity
Your work-stress triggers

- Use the questions above to identify your stress triggers. Write them down, and add any others that come to mind.

STRESS AT WORK, STRESS AT HOME

Are you keeping up? Do you need some help? If you've not already subscribed, why not try the daily text messaging service for extra encouragement and support. Just text 'Mellow 81' to 80881 now.

Each set of messages costs £1.50. Please see page xii for full terms and conditions.

Work-stress solutions

> **Today you will learn ...**
>
> to deal with the problem.

One of the worries employees have when they attempt to reduce stress overload is that they may end up achieving less than they need in order to keep their jobs.

Keeping your job is a necessity (unless you decide to change it – see Day 84), but these solutions will make you more productive, not less.

In order to reduce stress at work, you will need to do either one, two or all of the following:

◆ Deal with the specific stressors (get more organised, speak to your boss regarding work overload, speak to the unhelpful colleague).
◆ Challenge your views about your work (that you are not good enough to cope with the challenges, that others don't help you enough, that you get taken advantage of by your boss).
◆ Work on being less tense and on relaxing more when you are in a stressful situation (use good breathing skills, relaxation skills, get some fresh air, ensure you eat a healthy lunch).

We have covered all these areas in this book, so be sure that you use them in the workplace when you need them.

Here are some further solutions to workplace stress that include skills we have previously looked at.

Set realistic work goals

This will incorporate writing down what you can **realistically** achieve each day, by the end of the week and, of course, longer term, larger goals. You will then need to make a time plan to ensure you can achieve these.

Learn to negotiate

When you find yourself in conflict with your boss or your colleagues, you need to negotiate a solution that everyone is happy with. Using the assertiveness skills you have learned, remember to:

◆ Acknowledge the other person's position
◆ State your own, and the problem it creates
◆ Offer a 'win–win' solution that will hopefully benefit both parties.

Learn to delegate

Resist the temptation to do every task yourself. Maybe your colleague won't do it quite as well as you to start with, but they will learn.

Learn to say 'No'

If you don't have enough time, you don't have enough time. Saying, 'Yes' to something that you cannot possibly complete to the required standard in the time available will simply cause you further stress. Learn to say 'no'.

Limit your working hours

Working long hours is less productive than you think – as is working without a break. The longer we work without a break, the slower our productive output progressively becomes.

Improve your interpersonal skills

Poor working relationships can cause untold stress – especially in these days of open–plan offices, where many people are thrown together. Make a determined effort to charm even the most difficult colleague – the more people like you the more they will be willing to help you out, and make your own working day easier.

TOP TIP

- Achieving a reduced-stress or stress-free work environment involves identifying and changing your personal stressors, challenging your negative thinking about events, and working on relaxing your body.
- Think of delegating, saying 'No' more often.

Activity Stress-free working

- Pick just one of what are probably several personal stressors in your job. Using the suggestions above, think about what you might do to reduce or eliminate this stressor.

- Now put your ideas into practice.

STRESS AT WORK, STRESS AT HOME

Knock work-stress on the head at home

Today you will learn ...

to reduce work-stress even away from work.

You can do a great deal to relieve work-stress outside your place of work. This means making yourself as stress resilient as possible before you walk through the door.

Start your working day the previous evening

Go to bed in good time. When you work a long day, get home late, and feel cheated out of 'me' time, it is a temptation to grab it back by staying up late. This is natural and understandable – but don't do it. Set yourself a deadline for going to bed, and stick to it, or you will not function well the following day.

Get up earlier

Once you have got to grips with going to bed in good time, why not get up a little earlier? An alarm clock that rings at 7.00 am is no more of a shock than one that goes off at 7.20 am, but an extra tranche of time before you leave for work will ensure that you are relaxed, rather than rushed, when you finally step outside your front door.

Eat breakfast

When you get up in the morning, your body has gone for many hours without food at all – refuel to give it a chance to support you through the day ahead. Make sure you have breakfast, and that it is fuel-packed – wholegrain cereal, fruit, eggs, orange juice – rather than coffee and a croissant with a sugar content that will actually slow you down rather than speed you up. Give your body a chance.

Physical exercise

Exercise before work is a horrible thought! However, once you give it a go you will discover that it wakes you up and makes you feel very energised, rather than tiring you out. We are not necessarily suggesting an hour in the gym – instead you could walk the dog, walk to work, or get off the bus one stop earlier and walk the last section. If you drive, could you park a little further away? Do you walk to the station? Think about anything you can do to wake your body up with some form of exercise before you sit down in your office. At the very least, do a few minutes of stretching exercises when you get up.

STRESS AT WORK, STRESS AT HOME

Sunday night stress

'Sunday evening blues' are very common. If you suffer from this, make sure that Sunday evening is a relaxing, happy time. Sunday evenings can become stressful because not only are we acknowledging the end of the weekend and return to the grind the next day, but we often save up all our unpalatable chores until then – cleaning shoes, ironing clothes, paying the bills. Don't! Make Sunday evenings a haven of pleasure. Cosy up, rent a DVD, plan a nice supper, open a bottle of wine. Begin to look forward to Sunday nights.

Travelling to work

Commuting can be a major stressor. It can mean we arrive at our place of work tired, fractious and already in a bad mood before the working day has started. Think about:

◆ Catching a train/bus that is one earlier than you really need so that you can enjoy the journey rather than stress about delays
◆ Add extra time if you drive to work so that traffic jams are not stressors
◆ If you are in a train, make sure that you have something to read or listen to that is enjoyable
◆ In the car, find a good radio station or ensure you have a favourite CD with you. If you have little time to read, why not get hold of an audio cassette of a book on your 'to read' list, and listen as you drive?

⊙ TOP TIP

◆ You can make a real difference to your working day by making the non-working part a stress-free zone.

Activity

De-stress at home

● In your notebook, list each of the headings above, and leave some writing space underneath. Now jot down at least one good idea for a positive change you could make in each of these areas.

STRESS AT WORK, STRESS AT HOME

Getting the respect you deserve

> **Today you will learn ...**
>
> about respect.

Being both respected and respectful can have a great impact on a stressful work environment. Many people cite office politics as a huge trigger for stress, often feeling that the backbiting and manoeuvring of others is something outside of their control and yet extremely upsetting.

However, there are a variety of things you can do to generate what we might call a 'respectful environment'. These actions will minimise the stress created via work colleagues.

Your focus is to become the kind of person others really like to have around.

Never excuse mistakes that you make

Don't make excuses, and don't point the blame elsewhere. Everyone understands genuine cock-ups (we all make them from time to time) and has respect and admiration for the person who takes full responsibility for what has happened.

Give credit where credit is due

Conversely, don't attempt to steal anyone else's thunder. Give credit where credit is due, and praise others' good work, even where it shows up the fact that you did not think of it / do it yourself.

Treat everyone in the same way

One of the best pieces of advice we could give, with regard to getting on well with the wide variety of people you come across in a working environment, is never treat anyone either as superior or inferior to yourself.

Don't be a gossip

It is natural to want to chat about the day-to-day goings on in an office. However, don't become part of the office rumour machine, as you will lose the trust and respect of your peers. When chit chat starts, ensure that you:

◆ Don't say anything detrimental
◆ Don't agree with hearsay
◆ Remain impartial
◆ Say so, if you know that something said is definitely untrue.

Don't make promises you cannot keep

It is always tempting to be the White Knight who sorts out the problems of others, agrees to meet deadlines that are important, and offers to help all and sundry. However, if you cannot keep your word, your fall from grace will be worse than if you had honestly admitted that you simply could not do this or that in the first place.

Learn to listen

Don't be too eager to tell others how to solve their problems. Give them the space and opportunity to talk things through with you first, and to tell you how they feel about whatever has come up.

TOP TIP

◆ Don't become the office gossip.

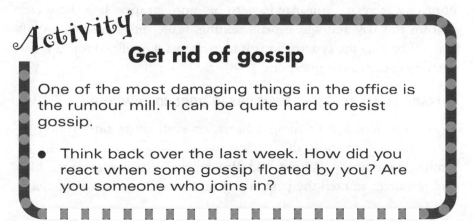

Activity

Get rid of gossip

One of the most damaging things in the office is the rumour mill. It can be quite hard to resist gossip.

● Think back over the last week. How did you react when some gossip floated by you? Are you someone who joins in?

STRESS AT WORK, STRESS AT HOME

Destructive distraction

'It's just impossible to get any work done in my office – there are so many distractions.' This is a common complaint, and hugely stressful. You will usually find that, of the many workplace

> **Today you will learn ...**
>
> not to be driven to distraction by distraction.

stressors that people find hard to deal with, distraction and interruption come out either at the top, or near the top, of their lists.

Questions, questions

Look back over the last day or so. How many times did you answer questions from others? How much time did you take to give each answer? If you multiply one by the other, you may get a shock when you realise how much time you give up in, say, a week, to answering questions from colleagues.

If this is a problem for you, then you need to become disciplined about answering.

Free period

One solution is a 'free period' each day, where you hang a sign on your door that says, 'Strictly no interruptions please', or you advise your secretary to hold all calls and not let anyone in. If you don't have a door or a secretary, you may have to be more creative. It is also a fact that, in this day and age, e-mail, texting, faxes and voicemail are all ways of beating the system. So you may need a disciplined formula for answering electronic questions.

Questions where the answer lies in print somewhere

Don't dig around your filing cabinet, or even waste time trying to recall the information the person wants. Simply direct them to Archives, Company Policies and Procedures or other manuals, files and resources and tell the person to find the information themselves.

STRESS AT WORK, STRESS AT HOME

Can anyone else answer the question?

Deflect, deflect, deflect! Tell the questioner who might be able to answer that question for them and leave it at that.

Monosyllabic responses

If it is possible to answer a question with 'Yes' or 'No', do so. Don't elaborate unless it is imperative.

Economies of scale

Where you have no choice but to answer fully, be economic. Avoid being chatty, simply give the information required.

Smile

All of the above solutions may be accepted with grace where you smile at the same time.

Other interruption beaters

- ◆ Screen your calls – either via a secretary or an answer machine. Caller ID will let you know who is calling.
- ◆ Use e-mail rather than telephoning.
- ◆ Learn to screen out noise by using distraction, focusing on what you are doing, or simply humming along with it. Don't allow yourself to become irritated by it.

TOP TIP

- • Plan to defeat interruptions and distraction using a variety of skills.

Activity **Reduce distractions**

- • What distracts or interrupts you most in your workplace? Having read the ideas above, what can you now do about this to reduce it?

STRESS AT WORK, STRESS AT HOME

Relationship rescue

One of the casualties of being under stress generally can be the quality of our personal relationships. Develop an awareness of how you react to those you love when you are stressed – do you become more aggressive and argumentative, or withdrawn, refusing to talk things through at all?

> **Today you will learn ...**
>
> how to keep your relationship in good shape when stress threatens it.

It may even be that your poor relationship skills are the cause of your stress.

Dealing with conflict

All relationships contain elements of conflict, and it is how these are resolved that will decide the quality of the relationship. Under stressful circumstances, you may lose your ability to relate in a loving and mature way. Disagreement is healthy – don't worry about it. Learning the skills of resolution so that everyone feels happy at the end of it is what matters.

Insisting on being right

When we feel upset or poorly treated, we often think that a way to feel better is to prove that we're right and that our partner is wrong.

In blame mode, you no doubt feel that you are being more than fair, and your partner is being totally unreasonable. In order to prove how right you are, you drag up every piece of evidence you can find to show that your partner is wrong. Why are you doing this? What outcome are you hoping for? Is this a win-win approach? When you are in conflict, think, all the time, in terms of outcomes and results.

Effective communication

How can you communicate effectively when you are stressed, distressed, upset – and certain you are right? Again, think in terms of

STRESS AT WORK, STRESS AT HOME

outcomes and results. Now answer the following question – and write your answer down.

Would you rather be right or be happy?

If your answer was 'be happy' then consider the following:

◆ When engaged in conflict with your partner:
 – Be assertive, not aggressive.
 – Acknowledge their point of view before expressing your own.
 – Make your goal to find a solution that you are both happy with.
 – Let your partner speak, and listen attentively. Don't simply wait impatiently for them to stop – or interrupt them – so that you can fire your next shot across their bows.
◆ Ask yourself what is likely to happen if you continue to insist on being right and blaming your partner.
◆ Remember the importance of **tone** when you are expressing grievances. Speak calmly and your partner will listen to what you have to say.

◎≡ TOP TIP

◆ Practice effective communication, and take note of the way you say things, as well as the content.

Activity

How do you deal with disagreement?

● In your notebook, write down four different communication methods that you use when dealing with conflict with your partner. For example, remaining calm, getting cross.

● If your four points are negative, write underneath what changes you will focus on making to get a better result from any future disagreements.

STRESS AT WORK, STRESS AT HOME

187

Owning your feelings

Relationship problems can cause a great deal of stress. Stress can cause us to react in an angry or inappropriate way to our partner's perceived demands and criticisms.

> **Today you will learn ...**
>
> to say 'I' instead of 'You'.

We usually feel, however, that it is our partner who has made us angry, upset, unvalued, inferior, perhaps even unloved. We are not to blame for this negative outburst – they made us do it.

CASE STUDY

Jim was helping Marie with the housework on Saturday morning. Domestic routine was not Jim's strong point – a messy house was fine by him. So he tended to work without especial enthusiasm, and rather slowly. Marie got crosser and crosser, and more and more critical of Jim's feeble efforts. Eventually, she exploded. 'You make me **so** angry – you make no effort at all – look at all the mess still in the kitchen you have supposedly tidied.' Jim retaliated with, 'Well, you make me feel useless. You criticise my efforts, you tell me everything I do is wrong. You make me feel like not bothering at all. What's the point?'

With that, Jim walked out of the house, leaving Marie fuming and upset – and with a lot of housework now to do on her own.

The problem for Jim and Marie was that each felt that the other had 'made' them feel as they did – angry in Marie's case, useless and resentful in Jim's.

TOP TIP

- Remember that no-one else can make you angry, distressed, resentful – or any other emotion. You choose it yourself.

STRESS AT WORK, STRESS AT HOME

It can be very difficult to control your emotions – but you **do** have control. Emotions are not reflex actions, like a knee jerk, or blushing, they are simply responses, and we can choose to what extent we activate them.

This idea is extremely important, as it stops us from criticising our partners. There is all the difference in the world between hearing 'You make me so angry when you do that' and 'I feel very angry when you do that', or between 'You really hurt me, saying such awful things to me' and 'I feel hurt when you say things like that.'

If you practise owning your emotions, not blaming the other person for them, the rewards will be enormous. Your partner will not feel criticised or blamed, but will be able to understand your feelings. This works in exactly the same way if your partner adopts the ownership of his or her feelings.

TOP TIP

◆ Once you take responsibility for how you feel and react, you can begin to talk more closely to your partner, and develop real intimacy.

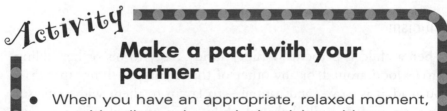

Activity

Make a pact with your partner

● When you have an appropriate, relaxed moment, consider discussing today's advice with your partner. Explain that you are planning to practise rephrasing what you say in order to take ownership of your feelings.

STRESS AT WORK, STRESS AT HOME

Stress-free parenting

Developing stress-free parenting techniques cannot be covered in one day, but the following tips are included as a positive step forward for those readers who have children.

> **Today you will learn ...**
>
> a few suggestions for those of you who are stressed out parents.

You may find that, when your stress levels go down, you will be able to improve your parenting even further without drastic action. If not, there are plenty of useful books out there.

Consistency

At the heart of good parenting, consistency rules. Children actually prefer a tight framework within which to operate. It makes them feel secure and relaxed – but the framework needs to be the same all the time. Every time you find yourself thinking, 'I can't be bothered to be firm' or 'It's just easier to give in' – please think again. If you are consistent, all children learn quickly and easily. Once you abandon that (even just **one** time) the child learns that he or she can turn the situation around if he or she is willing to fight enough, scream enough, argue enough. It is actually not his or her fault. They are simply learning what the boundaries are. Make sure they are always the same.

Criticism

When a child is perpetually rude, untidy, nasty to his or her sibling, throws food around, or any other of the myriad of things that drive you mad, it is easy – and natural – to lay in to them with criticism. 'You are such a badly-behaved child', 'No-one will like you' and various other harsh words will be on the tip of your tongue. You need, however, to think in terms of what results you want.

For example, Johnny's room looks like a pigsty, and you want him to tidy it up. Not just today, but on a regular basis. Here are two ways that you can put this to him. Which do you think will achieve the best **ongoing** result?

- 'Johnny, your room is disgusting and so are you. Get upstairs and tidy it straight away or no TV for you tonight.'
  Here, you are giving Johnny the clear impression that you are really angry with him and think he is a messy slob. He's likely to feel resentful and rebellious, and not at all like doing what he's asked.
- 'Johnny, you're usually so neat. It's not like you to have an untidy room.'
  Here, you are giving Johnny the impression that you are proud of his neatness, and quite puzzled by his untidy room. Also you are commenting on his behaviour without labelling him as 'disgusting'. He is more likely to think, 'Hey, Mum thinks I'm neat, so I should attempt to be that way.'

Listening and understanding

When a parent shows that they understand their child's feelings, the child feels soothed by the parent's comfort and concern. They feel nurtured, rather than isolated, and see their parents as understanding allies, to whom they can turn for comfort and support.

TOP TIP

- Children respond to consistent boundaries, which help them feel secure.
- Build praise into constructive feedback, which allows the child to respond positively.
- Focus on the behaviour without labelling the child or teenager.
- Listening and understanding can often calm a child down.

Activity

Be a better parent

- Which of the key skills above do you think you could incorporate into your own parenting style? Give them a go over the next few days, and note the results. Remember that, with children, the best response may not be immediate if they have been used to different signals from you, but persevere until you see more positive results.

STRESS AT WORK, STRESS AT HOME

Your notes

CHAPTER

10

BRINGING IT ALL TOGETHER

Becoming consciously competent

The final chapter in this book looks at developing stress-resilient habits. Many of them will seem like common sense, but actually incorporating these things into your life might require some effort. Possessing the tools is one thing – using them regularly is another.

> **Today you will review ...**
>
> the four stages of learning you need to go through to become competent.

There is good news, however. If you will make the effort, gradually you will find yourself doing these things naturally. They simply become part of your life.

Have you heard of the four stages of learning?

1. Unconsciously incompetent

This is where you would have been before you even thought of buying and reading this book. You probably accepted your stress as part of your life, and simply tried to cope with it as best you could, without much awareness of the idea of changing things.

2. Consciously incompetent

This stage is reached when you finally realise that things are not going well, and that you need to make some changes, but you are not quite sure how. You will have been at this stage when you decided to purchase this book.

3. Consciously competent

We hope that this is the stage you are beginning to reach now. At this point you are making changes, and they are (hopefully) making a difference, but unless you think about them, and focus, they don't happen. This is what being consciously competent means – it doesn't yet happen naturally.

This can be the stage at which many people give up. They are finding the work required too hard, and nothing happens without a lot of thought and effort. Like the gym membership you used every day, and now rarely bother with, or the diet you started with great hope, but which lasted only until you were offered a chocolate éclair – it's all too much.

4. Consciously competent

You're there! No more effort. Suddenly you find yourself doing the things that will allow you to live a relaxed, enjoyable, stress-free lifestyle, and you don't even have to think about it.

Keep the four stages of learning in your mind – for everything you attempt which is new and requires effort. They will hopefully encourage you to know that the major efforts are temporary, whilst the change for the better is permanent.

◎ TOP TIP

♦ Understanding the four stages of learning should increase your commitment to making an effort. It **will** come naturally in the end.

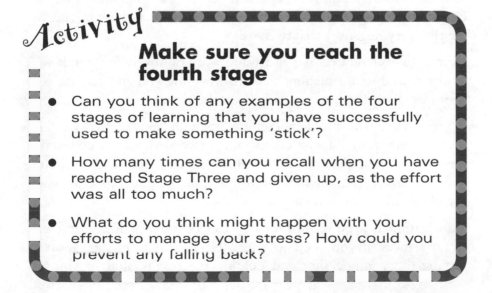

Activity

Make sure you reach the fourth stage

● Can you think of any examples of the four stages of learning that you have successfully used to make something 'stick'?

● How many times can you recall when you have reached Stage Three and given up, as the effort was all too much?

● What do you think might happen with your efforts to manage your stress? How could you prevent any falling back?

BRINGING IT ALL TOGETHER

Visualise it

We think in images more often than we realise. Here is an example.

You have decided to plan your holiday. Sitting in your lounge at home you and your partner browse through a variety of travel

Today you will review ...

how using imagery and visualisation can reduce stress and increase your confidence to deal with difficult situations.

brochures. Suddenly, your partner comes up with something. 'Listen to this' they say, and read a description of the desired holiday out loud to you. What is going through your mind at this moment? The chances are, you are visualising it. You will have pictures in your mind of golden beaches or snowy mountains, and you will almost certainly be visualising yourself within this picture – perhaps sipping drinks at a beach bar, or trekking across a mountain pass.

This is visualisation. We use it unconsciously a great deal.

For example, perhaps you feel you should be looking for a new job, then you focus on imagining yourself in the new employment situation you desire. It's similar to daydreaming!

When we are stressed, the images in our mind tend to be negative. We visualise ourselves failing to cope. It is almost like watching a video in our head – except that it is a video that has not been shot yet, and we are the (very negative) scriptwriters.

Here is an exercise to make visualising work positively for you. It will help you deal with situations that are worrying you and causing you stress, whether they are on-going or in the future.

If you have a real problem coming up with constructive ways of dealing with your difficulties, ask one or two friends or colleagues how they might deal with the same problem. You will find that everyone has at least one solution to offer, and you can construct your own best answer from these.

Visualisation is a powerful tool that can be used in many different circumstances. If you want to win a tennis match, picture yourself playing the winning shot and holding the trophy aloft. If you are

BRINGING IT ALL TOGETHER

going for a work promotion, imagine the boss shaking you by the hand and congratulating you on achieving it. The impact of imagery on your mental state is huge, and it is regarded as one of the most effective stress management techniques available for dealing with difficult situations.

Step 1	Think of a future situation that you are stressed about.
Step 2	Think about, or preferably write down, the aspects of the situation that are worrying you the most.
Step 3	Taking each difficulty one by one, think about how you might deal with each of them in a constructive way. It would be sensible to write down your ideas.
Step 4	Now visualise the situation. Imagine each difficulty you are worrying about coming up, and picture yourself coping with it as you have planned. Now repeat the process three or four times until it becomes easier to picture without effort.
Step 5	Keep this technique in mind and start using it regularly. Become aware of outcomes and how closely they match the visualisation you worked on.

Adapted from Palmer and Strickland (1996)

TOP TIP

- You can train your 'internal video maker' to produce films that give you images of positive outcomes. By replaying these videos in stressful situations, you will usually cope a great deal better.

Activity
Visualise success

- Think of a stressful situation that you will shortly have to deal with, and use the exercise above to identify the problems and solutions. Then visualise yourself putting the solutions into practice.

BRINGING IT ALL TOGETHER

De-stress by reducing worry

By worry and rumination, we mean the chronic 'niggling away' that goes on in our minds that can seem to override our best intentions to be positive, calm, relaxed and in control of our lives.

> **Today you will review ...**
>
> how to deal with repetitive worrying and rumination that is hard to dismiss.

How worry and rumination differ from our usual negative thoughts

You have already done a great deal of work on challenging negative thinking, and this is an excellent way of reducing stress. Rumination, however, is the longer-term, relentlessly ongoing result of specific thoughts. For example, you may hold very specific negative thoughts about a recent situation you think you dealt with very poorly. When you lie in bed at night ruminating, you will generalise this into a longer chain of 'I've never been much good at anything' thinking that is repetitive and self-focused. You will probably go back over all the instances in your life where you have failed – and once you have been through them once, you will go through them again and again until you do finally fall asleep.

Worry is very similar to rumination, with the exception that it tends to be about future events, rather than those in the past. Whilst specific negative thinking can be identified and challenged, generalised worry is like a dog with a bone – it will encompass a myriad of future possible situations and see gloom and doom in all of them.

Worry, worry, worry

How to deal with worry and rumination

If you cannot sleep at night because of these thoughts, or if you have a quiet moment in the day when you recall them, write down as many of them as you can remember. Once you have your list, look through it. Put a tick by any thoughts that seem to warrant attention (e.g. 'I really am getting more overweight than ever') and score through those that really have no merit (e.g. 'Supposing I never get a boyfriend?').

Now you can apply constructive thinking to the thoughts you have been having that you can do something about. You can also use visualisation as a good way of ridding yourself of unproductive worry and rumination – simply imagine yourself picking them up off the page and putting them into a waste bin.

You will need to practise the above a great deal before you can do it without thinking about it, but your efforts will be well rewarded.

TOP TIP

- Worry and rumination can dog our sleepless moments and increase our general stress levels. Sorting out which of these thoughts have value, and can be dealt with, and which need 'putting in the bin' will help you to reduce these problems.

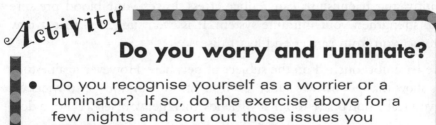

Activity
Do you worry and ruminate?

- Do you recognise yourself as a worrier or a ruminator? If so, do the exercise above for a few nights and sort out those issues you should be dealing with (helpful information) from those that need to be binned (useless information).

BRINGING IT ALL TOGETHER

Are you keeping up? Do you need some help? If you've not already subscribed, why not try the daily text messaging service for extra encouragement and support. Just text 'Mellow 91' to 80881 now.

Each set of messages costs £1.50. Please see page xii for full terms and conditions.

Connecting with others

> **Today you will review ...**
>
> the importance of good friendships.

Being in a state of stress can be isolating. When you feel you have too much to do, and too little time, you tend to focus on practical tasks, ticking them off your list as you race along. Yet one of the best ways of becoming resilient to stress is by connecting more with others.

Nurture your friendships

Ask people what they value most in life and it will almost certainly be family and friends. When people have regrets, it is often that they did not do more to nurture friendships, to spend more time with the people who mattered most to them.

Research has shown that those with a strong social support system are much more resilient to stress, and better able to deal with stress when it does arise.

What sort of social support system do you have? Opposite is a questionnaire for you to fill in to give you some idea of whether your support system is strong.

Cultivating friendships can reduce stress, lower your blood pressure and strengthen your immune system. It is even suggested that it may protect you from cancer and heart disease.

We have not touched on the subject of pets here. However, again, studies show that pet owners suffer less from stress than non-pet owners. So if you really don't have too many friends, then get yourself a cat or a dog!

TOP TIP

- Developing and nurturing your social support group will help to keep you stress-resilient.

Think of a situation which has caused you a great deal of personal stress. To what extent did each of the following help you with the problem?

1 = little support, 5 = a great deal of support

Husband/wife/partner	1	2	3	4	5
Mother	1	2	3	4	5
Father	1	2	3	4	5
Sister	1	2	3	4	5
Brother	1	2	3	4	5
Other relative	1	2	3	4	5
Close friend	1	2	3	4	5
Casual friend	1	2	3	4	5
Work colleague	1	2	3	4	5
Doctor/clergy/therapist	1	2	3	4	5

Add up your total score:
- 0–10: Low support
- 10–25: Moderate support
- 25–40: High support

Source: Cooper et al (1998)

Activity

Assess your support system

- Use your notebook to make a list of those people you could count on to be there for you if you were in difficulties.

- If the list is not very long, you may need to develop your friendships. Write a list of people you have perhaps lost contact with through not keeping in touch, and put a tick against any friendships that you feel you might like to renew. Now plan to write a letter or make a phone call to at least three of those people over the next month.

BRINGING IT ALL TOGETHER

'If you would take, you must first give, this is the beginning of intelligence.' Taoist principle

Do a good turn

One of the most common reasons for being stressed is a lack of time in which to accomplish the urgent tasks of life that need to be accomplished – usually with a tight deadline staring us in the face.

Today you will review ...

on how focusing on others can reduce stress.

The idea, therefore, that one could become less stressed by giving more time may not go down too well.

If you regard being stressed as equalling being unhappy, it makes sense to assume that becoming happier will equal feeling less stressed. Every piece of research into the conditions required and qualities needed to achieve happiness in life has shown that altruism is always at or near the top of the list. Psychologist Martin Seligman, in his book *Absolute Happiness* (2003) refers to, 'An astonishing convergence, across the millennia and across cultures' about this point.

Doing something for another person can greatly enhance your stress resilience. Simple acts of kindness and generosity can go along way.

This is how:

◆ You are less likely to be depressed and feel more satisfaction with the quality of your life.
◆ The fact that you are contributing to society in some way will give you a more positive outlook generally.
◆ Regular volunteer work can give you a sense of purpose.
◆ Even with little time to give, the sense of doing something worthwhile that gives meaning to our lives beyond simply looking after ourselves is a great stress-buster.
◆ Your sense of self-worth will increase.

Stress tends to multiply as our self-esteem reduces. Feeling good about ourselves counteracts this.

BRINGING IT ALL TOGETHER

Where do I begin?

This depends on what you find easiest a) regular, timed commitment, or b) simply having more of what we call 'other awareness' – literally thinking more about other people in general and what is going on in their lives, and looking for small ways in which you can help them. Or you can do both!

If you opt for the former, then bear the following in mind:

- ◆ Pick something that genuinely interests you
- ◆ Use your strengths. If you are a reasonable footballer, then offering to help, for example, disadvantaged children learn the game is a better use of your time than delivering food to older people
- ◆ Where you can, involve other family members, it will be more fun – and good for them as well.
- ◆ Don't over-commit yourself. It is better to start small and be consistent with your contribution.

TOP TIP

- ◆ 'Other awareness' is a concept you can develop and practise. The more you do kind acts for others, the more your self-esteem goes up – and stress levels will come down.

Activity
Help others and help yourself

- ● Spend some time today thinking about what you do for others. Do you consider that you have 'Other awareness' to any great extent?

- ● Use your notebook to start listing things that you might do – volunteering at your child's school, for example, or having more contact with a housebound or elderly neighbour.

BRINGING IT ALL TOGETHER

What are your hobbies?

Becoming stress resilient means taking time out for the following:

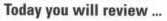

Today you will review ...

how hobbies can be stress busters.

◆ Creating a balanced life
◆ Having varied interests
◆ Ensuring that you build in relaxation time
◆ Focusing away from stressful thoughts by becoming absorbed in something non-stressful
◆ Having fun
◆ Being creative
◆ Stretching yourself without stress
◆ Looking to learn new things.

Which all adds up to – hobbies and interests!

What you do is not important, as long as it interests you, you get real pleasure from it and feel relaxed when doing it. Some hobbies have a social side – if you are a collector, for example, you may visit exhibitions or belong to a group of like-minded collectors. You might also decide to join a class to learn more about your hobby. Other activities, like gardening or painting, are regarded as very therapeutic because of the still and peaceful environment in which these interests are undertaken. You might, however, prefer something more raucous – becoming a member of a team sport should provide this sort of noisy camaraderie.

Consider how you spend your spare time, and whether becoming actively involved in something new that would provide pleasure and absorption could add to your life.

TOP TIP

◆ Hobbies and interests are excellent stress busters. They help enhance creativity and take our minds off our worries.

Activity
What are your interests?

● Do you already have one or more hobbies or interests?

● If you don't, jot down a few possibilities. Brainstorm some ideas and then review them. Is there anything in the list that you might like to give a go? Give consideration to what spare time you have, whether you like sedentary things or racing around, whether you prefer social hobbies or quiet solitude. Now pick one and write a brief action plan for how you are going to get started.

BRINGING IT ALL TOGETHER

Cultivate calm

Occasionally, reducing your stress in a way that involves very little effort is a necessity. Whilst we encourage you to learn various skills, techniques and lifestyle changes that will make a real

> **Today you will review ...**
>
> on how a small oasis of peace can work wonders.

changes that will make a real difference to your stress levels, we acknowledge that sometimes the very idea of thinking your way out of stress is just not what you can face in the moment.

Stress + tiredness = requirement for a peaceful place

Find a sanctuary (or two)

If you do not already have at least one place in your home – and possibly at work – that you can escape to when the demands on you and pressures around you are too great, then create one.

You will have a bedroom and a bathroom – and possibly a guest room. How often do people actually stay? Replace the bed with a sofa-bed and you are ready to create your own oasis.

You may have had a beauty treatment at a spa. Usually, the room that you are shown into whilst you wait for your massage, pedicure or whatever, is an oasis of tranquillity. Yet it is simply done, often in a tiny room – you can achieve the same at home. Some low lights, a few candles, soft music, a comfy chair or sofa. There is nothing more to it.

Take a bath

When we rush to get going in the morning, a quick shower is far more time effective than a bath. But it can become a habit. When did you last take a bath?

This is not about getting clean – this is about total relaxation in an oasis of calm.

- If you are in a family environment, book the bathroom for half an hour ahead of time, and tell everyone that they are not to disturb you.

- Make sure you have loads of hot water, a big fluffy towel and all the bath oils, soaps, face masks, eye masks, goat's milk treatments, etc. that you need.
- Turn off the bright light. Light half a dozen candles. Bring in a CD player and your favourite relaxing music.
- Lie back and close your eyes.

Really can't stay at home?

Too noisy, too cramped, too many people, phone calls, pets, etc? Have you ever been to your local park? Do you live within striking distance of a coffee shop or a book shop that has those lovely squidgy settees to sit on? Start thinking – you may have other local alternatives that will give you the peaceful moments that you need.

TOP TIP

- Sometimes, stress relief simply means quiet time in a peaceful place – create one for yourself, or find one not too far away.
- Discipline yourself to take time out to use it. Don't let the candles you purchased simply become an expensive waste of money.

Activity
Find your own oasis

- If you don't already have a sanctuary of any sort, now is the time to give some thought to making or finding one. Could you use any part of your home? What alterations would you need to make to achieve this? Where can you take time out in the workplace?

- Unless this is an anathema to you, plan a long, hot scented bath for your next free evening. Nip out to the candle/aromatherapy store and stock up first. Really relax and enjoy it – and then plan your next one.

BRINGING IT ALL TOGETHER

Take a break

Whilst this is an obvious stress
beater for some, a large number of
people tend to say, 'I am just too
busy to take a break,' or 'When I
go away, all I think about is work,
so there seems little point.'

Pre-planning

For busy, stressed people, holidays only happen with pre-planning. If
you are the kind of person who says, 'As soon as I see a free window,
I'm off,' it won't happen. You may need to plan far ahead, but **plan**.

Don't say, 'I just like to do things at the last minute.' That can mean,
'never'. Also, for stress reduction, one of the joys of a break is not just
the being on it, but the looking forward to it.

Who with?

Some of you will have families and friends as travelling companions.
However, we meet many people whose main reason for not going away
is, 'No-one to go with.' Join a group! This can be an interest group
(painting, sailing, hill walking) or a singles group (many tour operators
offer singles holidays in age groups, so that you will not be the only
Under 30 / Over 60). It can be daunting to show up on your own at
the airport or train station – but remember, it is the same for everyone,
and this will be an excellent opportunity to make new friends.

Where?

Choosing a holiday destination can be difficult. Keep a file through
the year of places you read about, or that a neighbour, friend or
work colleague tells you about, so that you have always got a choice
of places you want to go to and see. This gives you much more chance
of agreeing something with your partner than having only one
destination in mind.

TOP TIP

♦ Don't be vague about breaks. Build them into your life –
they are excellent stress-reducers.

Mini-breaks

For those who really do find it hard to relax away from work for more than a few days, the idea of mini-breaks has really taken off. Thursday to Monday usually means people hardly notice you are not there, which makes it much easier to get away.

For the most stress-reducing breaks, consider:

- A spa weekend. Look in the paper for bargain breaks – spa hotels love you at weekends when all the executives have gone, and this is reflected in the lower prices.
- Walking holidays are excellent de-stressors. Plan your own, or get in touch with a company that plans walking tours. Again, these holidays provide an opportunity to make new friends as well.
- A weekend either on or close to water is hugely relaxing. Either hire a boat, or stay by a lake and walk, sail, row or peddle.
- Painting breaks are renowned for their therapeutic qualities (even if you cannot paint at all – it really doesn't matter, and you will learn).
- Head off to the countryside and stay in a pretty inn.
- Continental weekend city breaks are fascinating. List the cities you would like to explore – Prague, for example, is wonderful – and book it.

Activity

Plan your breaks

- Do you have any holiday plans?

- If not, make a plan right now for at least one long weekend away within the next twelve weeks. Give some thought to the one after that as well, so that this becomes a regular feature of your year, not just a one-off. Write your plans down and show them to someone. Ask that person to check back with you regularly to see that you are achieving this.

BRINGING IT ALL TOGETHER

'Live not one's life as though one had a thousand years, but live each day as the last.' Marcus Aurelius

Knowing what is really important

Stress is often the result of not achieving the things we feel are important.

> **today you will review ...**
>
> how to reduce the stress in your life by assessing your values.

What we consider to be important is very much the product of our personal values and attitudes. However, we often give little or no time to consider what these are. We often inherit our parents' views rather than developing our own.

If we find our lives full of stress and unhappiness, we need to review our sense of perspective. What are we attempting to achieve in our lives? Is this consistent with the values and attitudes we have? Do we need to make changes so that there is a correlation between the two?

You need to clarify what your values are, and look at whether you are achieving what to you is important. Do the test opposite to get an idea of what really matters to you.

Look at the statements you gave a 3 score to. This will tell you a great deal about your values.

The important question to ask yourself now is, 'Is my way of life in line with my values?' If your answer is 'No', here is another cause of your stress.

TOP TIP

- ◆ Your values and attitudes play a large role in determining your stress levels. To become stress-resilient, your lifestyle and your values need to match as closely as possible.

Where 0 = not important at all to me, and 3 = extremely important to me, rate the following values:

Rating

- Achieving financial success _____
- Being the best at things I do _____
- Looking good physically _____
- Having a close family _____
- Others seeing me as successful _____
- Others seeing me as kind and trustworthy _____
- Having lots of friends _____
- Having total control at work _____
- My children being high achievers _____
- Spending some of my time helping others _____
- Having plenty of time to relax _____
- Having hobbies and interests outside work. _____

You need to make changes now, to ensure that the life you are living is consistent with the values you most believe will bring you happiness.

Activity

Does your lifestyle match your values?

- Make sure you find time to take the test above. Do the results show that your values and lifestyle work in harmony? If not, you will now need to think seriously about what changes you might make – which might involve changing your work, your social life or your personal life.

- Write down what these changes might be, and what you will do to activate them. Refer back to what you have written in a month's time, and see what progress you have made.

BRINGING IT ALL TOGETHER

That's funny – appreciating humour

That laughter is the best medicine is well known. However, most of the time, when stressed, harassed, rushed and anxious, we simply forget about it. There simply doesn't seem very much to laugh about.

> **Today you will review ...**
>
> the power of humour to relieve stress.

This isn't actually true. Many of the hassles and inconveniences of life offer you the option of either driving yourself insane or of seeing a funny side. It simply requires looking at things hard, and in a certain way.

Don't be too serious

Taking life too seriously is a mistake, unless you want your stress levels to rise. Humour will increase your stress-resilience and enable you to relax a lot more.

Much stress comes from giving too much importance to how you see yourself. Find a funny side to defuse difficult situations and you will get others laughing with you. We tend to think someone has a good sense of humour when they laugh at the same things we laugh at.

Humour as good medicine

Humour will:

◆ Relax your body
◆ Increase your immunity
◆ Give you a calmer, more positive perspective.

Life **is** serious – but you can find humour if you look for it.

- Laugh at yourself more – become self-effacing. Telling things in a way that makes you look slightly idiotic is both endearing and gives others a chance to laugh with you. This really is a quality to cultivate.

- Spend more time with funny people and notice what they find funny, how they tell stories, what they do in general to make others laugh.

- Start a humour scrap book. Whenever you read anything funny in a paper or magazine, cut it out and stick it in your book. When you hear a funny joke, record the punchline. You never know, you may even recall it at a good moment.

- Start a collection of films or TV series that have really made you laugh. Watching professionals using humour is an education in learning it yourself.

TOP TIP

- Using humour reduces our stress levels by bolstering our immune system and relaxing us in stressful situations.

Activity
Learn to laugh at yourself

- When did you last have a really good laugh? Why?

- If you are not someone who normally laughs at yourself, jot down in your notebook two or three recent occasions where things went wrong for you. Now ask yourself whether you could re-tell these disasters, putting a humorous spin on them? Get used to asking yourself this question and it will soon come naturally to you to make a comedy out of a crisis.

BRINGING IT ALL TOGETHER

When going it alone is too tough

Sometimes, in spite of our best efforts, the support of outside professional assistance may be an answer to relieving stress symptoms. Such external assistance can take the form of physical relaxation, alternative therapies or psychological therapies. All have their place, and you need to consider – possibly by trying different therapies out, or by asking for suggestions from friends and colleagues who have tried them – which is the best for you.

> **Today you will review ...**
>
> the different kinds of outside help available to help with stress relief.

Physical therapies

Massage

When it comes to alleviating stress – at least for a period of time – massage rates very highly. Its virtues as a de-stressor are many:

- It will help you sleep better.
- It can boost your immune system.
- It reduces the hormones that encourage stress.
- It increases serotonin levels – the feel-good brain chemical.
- It can reduce your blood pressure.
- It feels blissful whilst you are having it!

Alternative therapies

Acupuncture

Practised in Asia for more than 5,000 years, acupuncture aims to release the flow of energy that can be blocked by stress. It is a therapy now recognised by the World Health Organisation, and there is a growing body of evidence that its healing powers for a variety of ailments, including stress, are considerable.

Reflexology

Reflexology advocates that the underside of your foot is a miniature representative of your body as a whole. Working with a detailed diagram that relates areas of the foot to areas of the body, the reflexologist manipulates the foot, working to both soothe and relieve the corresponding troubled area of your body.

Cranial osteopathy

The focus of cranial osteopathy is to apply light pressure to the head and body to encourage the release of stress and tension and to encourage a relaxed state of mind and body.

Aromatherapy

Scents really do make a difference. Aromatherapy has been used throughout history in the East, and is now gaining wider acceptance in the Western world. Aromas work because they trigger the brain to release neurotransmitters (chemical messengers), which control blood pressure, breathing, heart rate — and stress levels. Whilst you have the option of visiting a professional aromatherapist, most health-food stores sell a variety of essences that you can use at home if you prefer.

TOP TIP

◆ There is a wide variety of professional help available to relieve stress, both physical and psychological. You may want to try two or three to see which help you the best.

Activity Get some help

● Have you ever considered or tried any of the therapies discussed above?

● If not, in the light of knowing how helpful they can be in reducing stress levels, are there any that you would be willing or interested in trying out now? We suggest you research two or three, then pick one and book an appointment. (see Appendix on page 221)

BRINGING IT ALL TOGETHER

Mayo and coffee

When events in your life seem almost too much to handle, when 24 hours in a day are not enough, remember the mayonnaise jar and two cups of coffee.

Today you will review ...

the importance of putting events in perspective.

A professor stood before his philosophy class with some items in front of him. Without saying a word, he picked up a very large, empty mayonnaise jar and proceeded to fill it with golf balls.

He then asked the students if the jar was full. They agreed that it was.

The professor then picked up a box of small pebbles and poured them into the jar. He shook the jar lightly. The pebbles rolled into the open areas between the golf balls.

He then asked the students again if the jar was full. Again, they agreed that it was.

The professor next picked up a box of sand and poured it into the jar. Of course the sand filled up everything else.

He asked once more if the jar was full. The students responded with a unanimous 'Yes'.

The professor then produced two cups of coffee from under the table and poured the entire contents into the jar, effectively filling the empty space between the sand.

The students laughed.

'Now,' said the professor, as the laughter subsided, 'I want you to recognise that this jar represents your life. The golf balls are the important things – your family, your children, your health, your friends and your favourite passions – things that, if everything else was lost and only they remained, your life would still be full. The pebbles are the other things that matter, such as your job, your house and your car. The sand is everything else – the small things. If you put the sand into the jar first,' he continued, 'there is no room for the pebbles or the golf balls.'

'The same goes for life. If you spend all your time and energy on the small things, you will never have room for the things that are important to you. Pay attention to the things that are critical to your happiness. Play with your children. Take time to get medical check-ups. Take your partner out to dinner. Play another 18 holes of golf. There will always be time to clean the house and mend the broken chair. Take care of the golf balls first – the things that really matter. Set your priorities. The rest is just sand.'

And the coffee?

One of the students raised her hand and inquired what the coffee represented. The professor smiled. 'I'm glad you asked. It just goes to show you that no matter how full your life may seem, there's always room for a couple of cups of coffee with a friend.'

TOP TIP

- ◆ Stress can be caused by our worrying far too much about things that don't deserve that level of importance – focus less on the small things, and enjoy those which are really important to you.
- ◆ Remember to make time for your friends.

Activity
What really matters?

Take a quiet moment to spend five minutes doing this test.

- ● You get some bad news. You are told that you only have a few months to live. What will you miss the most? Perhaps seeing your children grow up? Perhaps the blue sky and the countryside around you? This will give you an idea of what is really most important to you.

- ● Write these down. Now write down all the things that have caused you stress in the last week, and put ticks against the ones that seem to really matter, in the light of the above.

- ● We hope you have very few ticks!

BRINGING IT ALL TOGETHER

'One does not leave a convivial party before closing time.'
Winston Churchill

And finally – get a life!

To have a truly stress-resilient lifestyle, you need to ensure that you have a balanced life with variety in it.

> **Today you will learn ...**
>
> to do just that.

Stop and take a look at your life. The chances are, if you are seriously stressed, that your life is either:

◆ Too hectic, with more crammed into it than it is possible for Superman to achieve

◆ Too one-dimensional – possibly involving too much work with little time for anything else, or too stereotyped, with everyday routines for each day of the week that mean there is no room for new and exciting experiences.

Perhaps you are not quite sure what is missing. The questionnaire below will show you whether you have enough balance in your life to keep you stress resilient.

Tick those which apply to you.

- I enjoy my work but don't work ridiculous hours or take it home with me. ☐
- I have at least one or two hobbies and interests that I enjoy. ☐
- I have great friends and see them regularly. ☐
- I have a supportive family. ☐
- I take at least one holiday each year. ☐
- I spend some of my time helping others. ☐
- I don't have particular money worries. ☐
- I have strong religious/spiritual beliefs. ☐
- There are always two or three things in the week that I really look forward to. ☐
- I love trying new things and meeting new people. ☐
- I see the funny side of most things. ☐
- I consider my life to be fairly well-balanced. ☐

Less than 4 ticks = You don't really 'have a life' in the best sense of the phrase. You will need to work hard on adding more variety and positively pleasurable areas to your life if you are to become truly stress-resilient.

4–8 ticks = There is room for improvement. Look again at those points you have failed to tick and think about how you might incorporate them into your life.

9–12 ticks = You have 'got a life', and there is little more to do other than enjoy it – and ensure that you keep it that way.

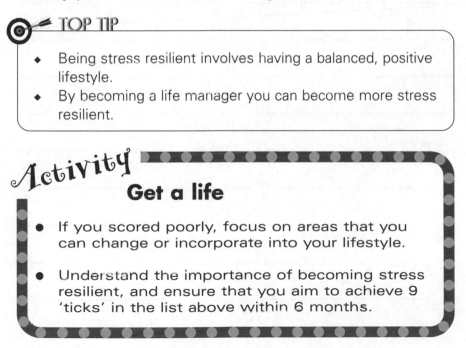

TOP TIP

- ◆ Being stress resilient involves having a balanced, positive lifestyle.
- ◆ By becoming a life manager you can become more stress resilient.

Activity

Get a life

- If you scored poorly, focus on areas that you can change or incorporate into your lifestyle.

- Understand the importance of becoming stress resilient, and ensure that you aim to achieve 9 'ticks' in the list above within 6 months.

BRINGING IT ALL TOGETHER

Your notes

APPENDIX

Psychological approaches

Counselling and psychotherapy

Stress can often be induced, or made worse, by crises in your life that you find hard to deal with (divorce, redundancy, bereavement or other personal difficulties), or by past events – possibly even in your childhood – that you have not dealt with and moved on from (feelings of low self-esteem caused by over-critical parents, for example).

Talking these issues through with a therapist who can help you come to terms with the past (usually called insight-based therapy) or who will help you discover solutions to your difficulties through changes you might make in your present thinking or circumstances (solution-focused therapy) may help you to eliminate the stress associated with these problems.

Life coaching

Where you feel that your stress is caused more by simply not being in control of your life, where you feel stuck in a rut that you cannot seem to get out of or where you really don't know what the best changes would be to make to your life, then Life Coaching will be able to help you.

This is a very goal-oriented approach. The coach will help you to define your goals and then work with you to ensure that you achieve them. In a sense, the coach is helping you to define more clearly what you want, and also to develop order out of chaos – this will result in a huge decrease in your stress levels.

USEFUL CONTACTS

The websites below provide information on a range of topics including stress management and health. Many of the organisations hold a register of qualified practitioners should you want coaching, counselling or therapy.

Association for Coaching
www.associationforcoaching.com

Association for Rational Emotive Behaviour Therapy
www.arebt.org

Association of Reflexologists
www.aor.org.uk

British Association for Counselling and Psychotherapy
www.bacp.co.uk

British Association for Behavioural and Cognitive Psychotherapies
www.babcp.org.uk

British Psychological Society
www.bps.org.uk

British Society of Experimental and Clinical Hypnosis
www.bsech.com

Centre for Stress Management
www.managingstress.com

Centre for Coaching
www.centreforcoaching.com

General Hypnotherapy Register
www.general-hypnotherapy-register.com

Health and Safety Executive
www.hse.gov.uk

International Stress Management Association (UK)
www.isma.org.uk

Institute of Health Promotion and Education
www.ihpe.org.uk

National Association for Holistic Aromatherapy
www.naha.org

The Meditation Society of Australia
www.meditatation.org.au
Provides free membership and a free online meditation course.

The British Wheel of Yoga
www.bwy.org.uk

United Kingdom Council for Psychotherapy
www.ukcp.org.uk

BIBLIOGRAPHY

L. Bilodeau, *The Anger Workbook* (Minnesota, Hazelden, 1992)

G. Butler and A. Hope, *Managing Your Mind* (Oxford, University Press, 1995)

B. Clegg, *Instant Motivation* (London, Kogan Page, 2000)

L. Cooper and S. Palmer, *Conquer Your Stress* (London, CIPD, 2000)

S. Covey, *The Seven Habits of Highly Effective People* (London, Simon and Schuster, 1992)

M. Davis, E. Eshelman and M. McKay, *The Relaxation and Stress Reduction Workbook* (Oakland, CA, New Harbinger, 2000)

W. Doherty, *Take Back Your Marriage* (New York, Guilford Press, 2001)

W. Dryden, *Overcoming Procrastination* (London, Sheldon, 2000)

W. Dryden, *Dealing with Difficulties in REBT* (London, Whurr, 1996)

W. Dryden, *Progress in REBT* (London, Whurr, 1992)

A. Elkin, *Stress Management for Dummies* (New York, Wiley, 1999)

T. Gillen, *Assertiveness* (London, CIPD, 1997)

D. Goleman, *Emotional Intelligence* (London, Bloomsbury, 1996)

G. Hargreaves, *Stress Management* (London, Marshall, 1998)

G. McMahon, *Coping with Life's Traumas* (Dublin, Newleaf, 2000)

G. Namie and R. Namie, *The Bully at Work* (Naperville, IL, Sourcebooks, 2003)

C. Padesky, *Mind Over Mood* (New York, Guilford, 1995)

S. Palmer and L. Strickland, *Stress Management: A Quick Guide* (Dunstable, Folens, 1996)

S. Palmer, C. Cooper and K. Thomas, *Creating A Balance* (London, British Library, 2003)

R. Potter-Efron, *Angry All the Time* (Oakland, CA, New Harbinger, 2004)

J. Robinson, *Communication Miracles for Couples* (Boston, Conari, 2000)

J. Ross, *The Mood Cure* (London, Thorsons, 2003)

M. Seligman, *Learned Optimism* (New York, Free Press, 1998)

M. Seligman, *Authentic Happiness* (London, Nicholas Brierley, 2003)

A. Wells, *CBT of Anxiety Disorders* (Sussex, Wiley, 2000)

Why not
try another title in the  GET A LIFE! series?

BONE IDLE to BODY IDOL
0-340-90799-1

MOODY to MELLOW
0-340-90801-7

DRAB to FAB
0-340-90804-1

SINGLE to SETTLED
0-340-90800-9